I0483365

Graces
Received

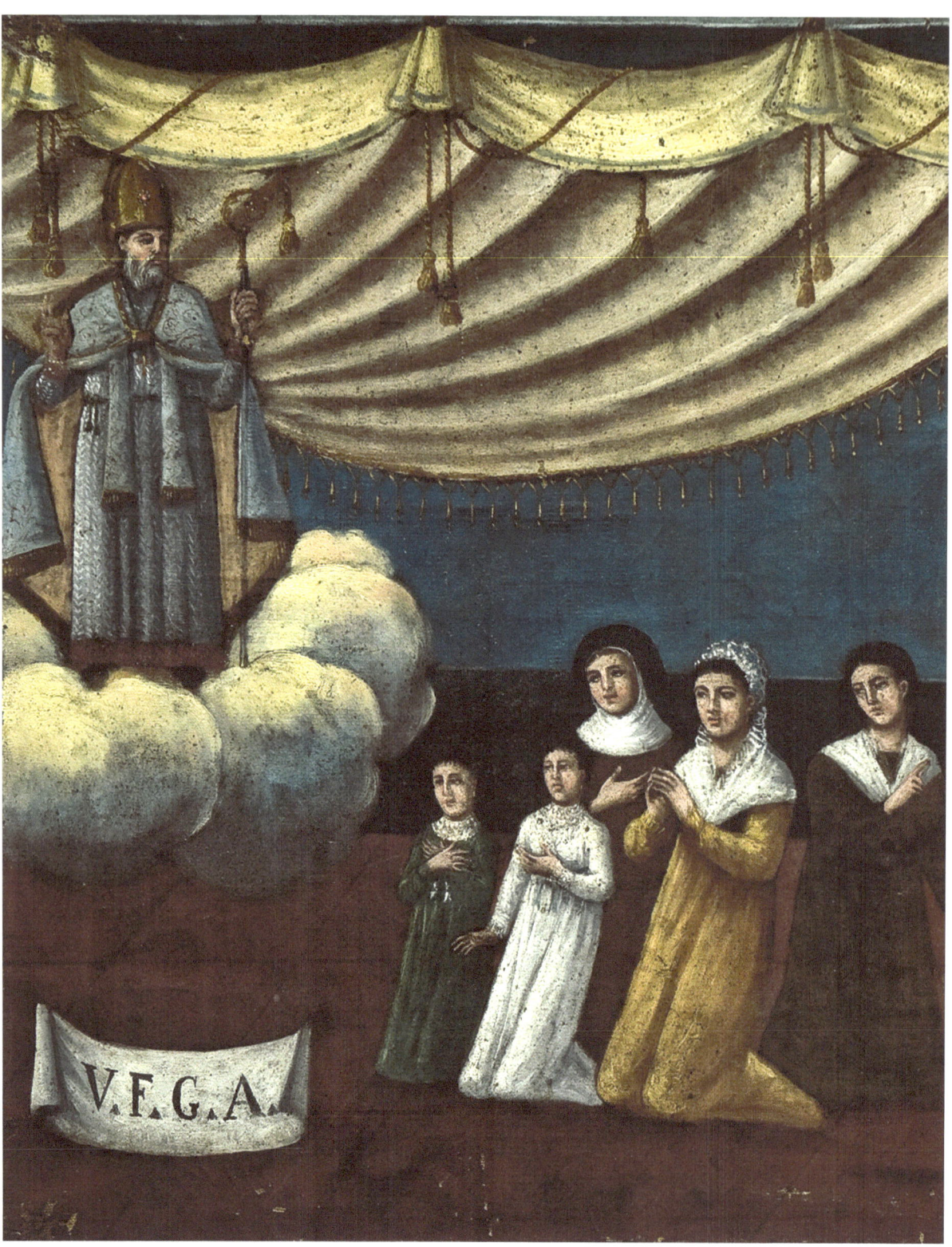

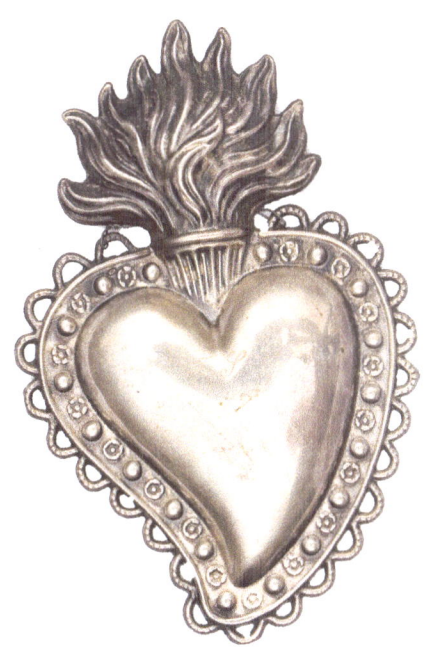

Graces Received

PAINTED AND METAL EX-VOTOS
FROM ITALY

THE COLLECTION OF LEONARD NORMAN PRIMIANO

EDITED BY ROSANGELA BRISCESE AND JOSEPH SCIORRA

JOHN D. CALANDRA ITALIAN AMERICAN INSTITUTE

QUEENS COLLEGE, CITY UNIVERSITY OF NEW YORK

2012

STUDIES IN ITALIAN AMERICANA | VOLUME 4
GRACES RECEIVED: PAINTED AND METAL EX-VOTOS FROM ITALY
THE COLLECTION OF LEONARD NORMAN PRIMIANO

©2012 BY THE AUTHORS
ALL RIGHTS RESERVED.
PRINTED IN THE UNITED STATES OF AMERICA

JOHN D. CALANDRA ITALIAN AMERICAN INSTITUTE
QUEENS COLLEGE, CUNY
25 WEST 43RD STREET, 17TH FLOOR
NEW YORK, NY 10036

ISBN: 978-0-9703403-7-5

LIBRARY OF CONGRESS CONTROL NUMBER: 2011940941

Cover: figure 5, detail

Frontispiece: figure 35, detail

Title page: figure 13

Design: Polly Franchini

Catalog photography: John Chew

Contents

Rosangela Briscese and Joseph Sciorra

THIS BOOK is the result of an exhibition by the same name that we curated at the John D. Calandra Italian American Institute's Manhattan gallery, which ran from September 2011 to January 6, 2012. The exhibition featured twenty-four paintings and twenty-nine metal ex-votos dating from 1832 to 1959 (all but four are reproduced here) from the private collection of folklorist and Religious Studies scholar Leonard Norman Primiano of Cabrini College. Both the exhibition and book emerged out of Primiano's and folklorist Joseph Sciorra's ongoing collaboration and professional interests in Catholic material culture and are in keeping with the mission of the Calandra Institute, a Queens College research institute, to foster and promulgate scholarly inquiry of Italian-American history and culture.

Collectively, the book's three essays address a set of specific issues: a general history of ex-votos and their place within Catholic thought, their creation and use by Italian Americans, and finally, the ex-votos' social life beyond their original religious context, in particular, as collectibles and inspiration for contemporary studio-trained artists. In this way, the authors seek to establish what anthropologist Igor Kopytoff calls the "cultural biography of things," that is, the varied meanings and values assigned an object in ever shifting contexts.

Given the indeterminate provenance of the items in Primiano's collection, as described in his essay, we are unable to provide the complete catalog descriptions for the paintings and metal ex-votos. All the artwork is unattributed except figure 39, which is signed by the artist "L. Maffa."

The production of this book, which took place in somewhat rushed circumstances, was, in and of itself, something of a miracle. Thus, in keeping with the ex-voto's expression of gratitude, we would be remiss not to offer our heartfelt thanks to several people whose hard work, dedication, and enthusiasm helped bring this project to fruition.

First and foremost, we thank Leonard Norman Primiano for helping to conceptualize the original exhibition and this book, and for lending his unique collection for its inaugural display at the Calandra Institute. His generosity, erudition, and keen sense of humor remain a constant source of inspiration.

Kate Wagle submitted her essay a month and a half after we invited her to participate in the project and expeditiously responded to all our editing questions. We are thankful for this opportunity to have met a new colleague.

We are grateful to designer Polly Franchini of Oronzo Editions who volunteered her services and delivered this stunning book in record time.

Our thanks to Ernestine Franco of Pern Editorial Services, who took on the task of copy editing the articles in the span of mere days; John Chew for his meticulous photographing of the artwork; and our colleagues at the Calandra Institute, Lisa Cicchetti, Rachel Hoyle, Gabrielle Pati, and Phyllis Tesoriero, who helped in the conceptualization and implementation of the exhibition and this book.

And finally, we wish to express our gratitude to Dean Anthony Julian Tamburri for leading with discernment and civility the Calandra Institute into new arenas of intellectual inquiry and for providing us with the opportunity and support to mount the exhibition and produce this book.

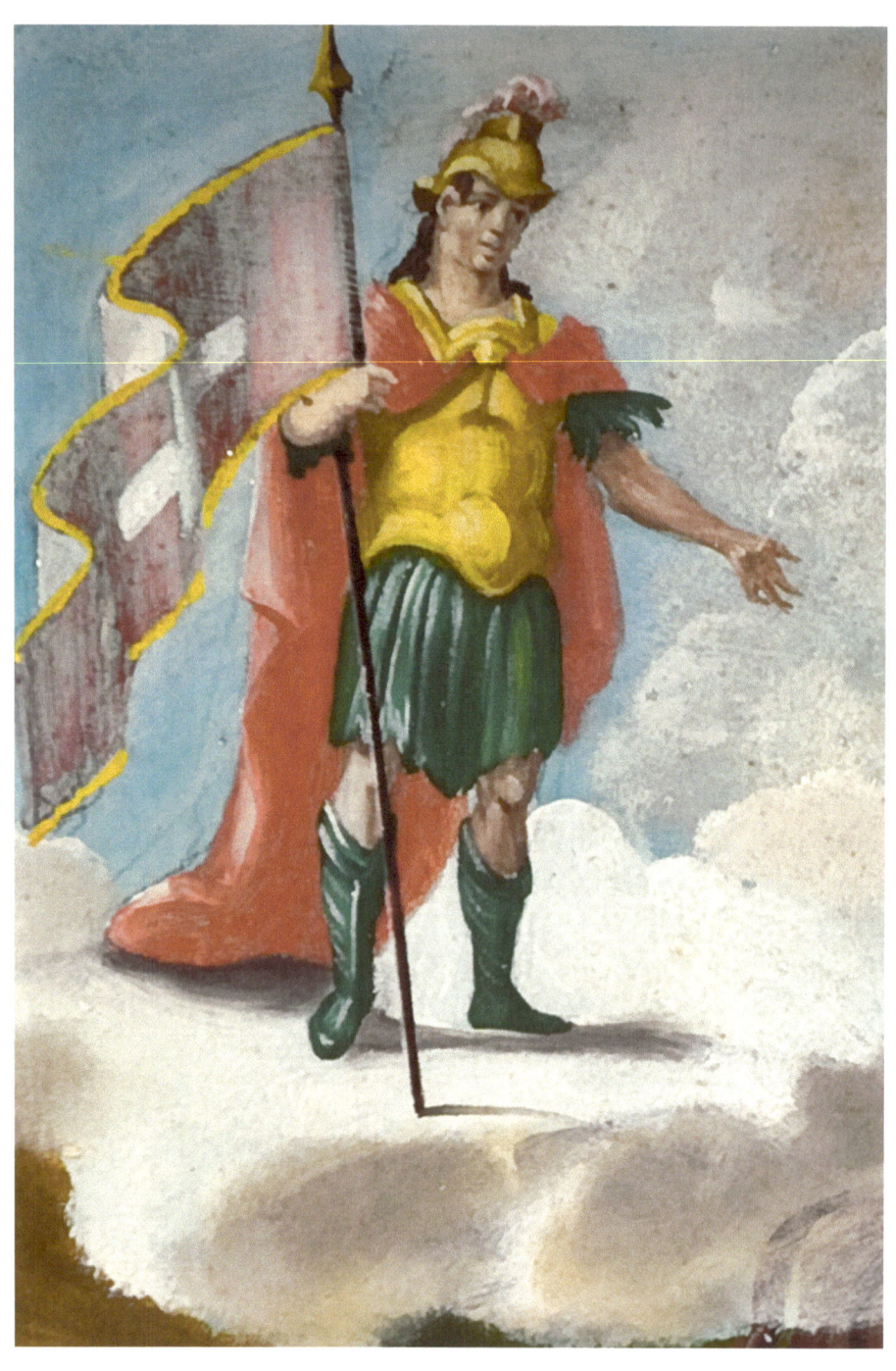

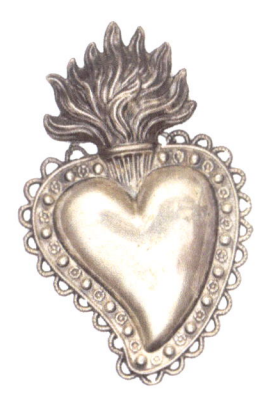

Catholiciana Unmoored

Ex-votos in Catholic Tradition
and Their Commercialization as Religious Commodities

LEONARD NORMAN PRIMIANO

Offer to God a sacrifice of thanksgiving, and pay your vows to the Most High. Call on me in the day of trouble;
I will deliver you, and you shall glorify me. (PSALM 50:14–15)

AN EX-VOTO is a voluntary offering to a saint or divinity. It is undertaken, performed, or dedicated in fulfillment of or in accordance with a vow and given in gratitude for a favor, blessing, or healing received. Synonymous with vow making, *ex-voto* is a Latin term, short for *ex voto suscepto*, "from the vow made" or "according to the promise that was made." The literal translation of *ex-voto* breaks down as follows: *ex* = from, in accordance with, or on account of; *voto* (the ablative form of *votum*) = vow, votive offering, prayer, desire, or hope; ex-voto, therefore, is most accurately translated as "in accordance with a vow or prayer."

In the material culture of Christianity, ex-votos can take various forms including carved or molded objects or painted panels. The destination of an ex-voto offering is a church, chapel, shrine, or oratory where the worshipper seeks grace or wishes to extend public gratitude. Ex-votos have had wide appeal for many centuries among many Christians, specifically Roman Catholics and Eastern Orthodox, throughout the world, especially Europe (e.g., Germany, Greece, Italy, Poland, Spain, Switzerland), parts of Asia (e.g., the Philippines), and Latin America (e.g., Bolivia, Brazil, Guatemala, Mexico, Peru, Puerto Rico) (see Francis 2007; Nolan and Nolan 1989, 71–78). Sites of Roman Catholic pilgrimage frequently contain any number of forms of ex-voto, from text-centered plaques, to miracle paintings, to floral arrangements, to crafted wax or wooden correspondences of body parts cured or protected by a saint, to silver hearts honoring the Sacred Heart of Jesus (see Carroll 1992, 83; Morgan 2008). Ex-votos can take the form of wooden houses, paintings of ships saved, or even models of

Opposite

Figure 21 (detail)

ships themselves. Jewelry or precious gems can be offered as ex-votos—as in the case of the icon at the shrine of the Black Madonna at Jasna Góra Monastery in Częstochowa, Poland, where mounds of amber necklaces adorning the walls of the chapel of the revered image are so resplendently abundant they resemble folds of orange fabric. In the last fifty years, the Catholic ex-voto tradition has changed to include more cost-effective means of vow fulfillment: mass-produced paper ephemera images of Jesus, Mary, and the saints; photographic portraits; and hand-written notes of those who need or were granted heavenly intercession.[1]

The term *ex-voto* represents a constellation of prayerful thoughts, devotional systems, artistic craft production, meaningful materials and symbols, ritual contexts, and social interactions (Faeta 2007, 60). When a Catholic prays for the intercession—the personal attention and demonstrated action—of a holy person to respond to human requests for assistance in daily life (to alleviate economic problems, attain a position of employment, maintain a relationship, or grant a healing), he or she can make a vow as a part of that plea for intercession. An ex-voto is the visible commemoration of the fulfillment of that request by the believer in gratitude to Jesus, the Virgin Mary, or a saint. Taking the form of an object of devotion, remembrance, declaration, or gratitude related to that prayer, it is the materialized expression—on painted metal or canvas, from hammered silver, tin, or gold, or in molded wax—of obligation or thanks to a saint or holy figure for a miraculous intervention, whether in the form of money, healing, or protection in the life of an individual. It can also be the commemoration of a battle during times of war or, equally serious, salvation from accidental injury or imminent death where, perhaps, in a second of desperation a loved one has called on a holy patron for assistance.

Bearing these definitional foundations in mind, this essay places ex-votos into historical and contemporary perspective within Christian spirituality and art, and especially as manifestations of Italian Catholic personal piety. To this end, I also explore how these expressions of vernacular Catholicism have been recontextualized in the digital age not as offerings or artistic expressions of personal faith but as objects detached from a ritual or devotional context and redefined as electronic auction items, coveted collectables, or "charming" handcrafted art.

Historical Developments

The practice of making and offering ex-voto objects is ancient and goes back at least as far as the Etruscans, the precursors of the Romans. While there were small offerings made in response to requests concerning health and fertility, votive offerings were also offered for other purposes as well. As far back as the Greek Geometric Period (ca.

900–700 BCE), small bronze figures of gods, animals, and people were made to be left as offerings in temples. It was also common practice among the Romans for military generals to vow the building or rebuilding of an entire temple in return for victory on the battle field.[2]

Within Christianity, there is a rich historical connection between the practice of ex-voto offerings and the rise of the cult of the martyrs and saints—that "spiritual elite whose holiness was recognized posthumously" (Nystrom and Nystrom 2004, 109); the tradition of saintly relic and tomb devotion; the concept of the patron saint and the human client—saintly protector relationships that developed in late antiquity (see Brown 1981). One of the most vivid expressions of the Christian saint cult was the honor paid to the miracle-producing physical remains, literally the sanctified bones, of these holy men and women. What made this belief in saints even more viable was that complementing the miraculous nature of relics—their bodily remains—was the sense of communion and communication that the saints retained as redeemed personalities in heaven with their Christian brethren on Earth. The apostle Paul had noted in his Epistle to the Romans (12:4–8) "so we, though many, are one body in Christ, and individually members one of another." It only seemed reasonable that, if living Christians prayed for each other, those individuals redeemed in heaven would do the same (Nystrom and Nystrom 2004, 109).[3] It was the duty of patron saints to act as heavenly intercessors at the time of an individual's judgment before God the Father or Jesus, as well as manifest earthly protection from the vicissitudes of a potentially violent and disease-filled world. The saint, however, expected the loyalty of his or her charges, which by the Middle Ages "was promised in a vow (votum) consummated in the form of a commendation" (Angenendt 2010, 24), some formal act that served to express the bond between patron and loyal follower. In his rich discussion of relics and their veneration in medieval Europe, Arnold Angenendt explains:

> In general, a gift of thanks for being saved was recommended, at least the gift of a candle, with the utterance of certain prayers, or the celebration of masses, at most a pilgrimage . . . . The formula for this was: *votum fecit–gratiam accepit*—the one who was saved has made a vow, and the saint has accepted it. Often one made votive offerings: an image of the person saved or of a healed body part; then objects associated with the rescue or images of them. In the ancient church, votive offerings had been forbidden; instead, a gift to the poor was expected. In the Middle Ages it had to be an offering to the saint . . . The figures of persons and their parts not only illustrated their healing, but also represented a "speaking" gift of thanks. (Angenendt 2010, 24)

By the late Middle Ages, votive images took on a visual pattern of familiarity and communication including the dangerous circumstance below on Earth—whether serious accident/situation or deadly illness—and the miraculous intervention marked by the presence of the saint or Virgin Mary above in the heavenly clouds (see Freedberg 1989, 136–60).

Within the Italian ex-voto tradition and in the Italian language, the common term for "object" ex-votos is *ex-voto oggettuale* or *miracolo* (miracle). The most common form of such an object resembles a piece of human anatomy: the anatomical ex-voto or *ex-voto anatomico* (Salvatori 2010, 26). In Italian, an ex-voto "painting," that is, the illustration in paint of a miracle story on a particular material/surface, is referred to either as *ex-voto*, or *tavoletta votive* (Carroll 1992, 82 refers to these paintings as *tavolette dipinti*).[4] In the specific case of Italian painted ex-votos, Mariolina Rizzi Salvatori offers a hierarchical explanation of their social origin and appeal, with the tradition originating in the fifteenth century through the commissions of wealthy patrons to artists. "According to a patron's wealth, the painting would then be hung in a church, private chapel, or home. When the tradition spread to the less wealthy, it fell out of fashion with the upper classes. From Italy the tradition spread to Europe, and eventually in the colonial period to Latin America, reaching its height in Mexico during the middle of the nineteenth century" (Salvatori 2010, 26; see also Carroll 1992, 84). In the Americas, especially Mexico, the best known, and most frequently found examples of such humble, small religious paintings on tinplate are known as *retablos* and *ex-votos*.

a rich historical connection between the practice of ex-voto offerings and the rise of the cult of the martyrs and saints

Within Mexican Catholic piety, "retablos were images of individual saints painted to adorn home or work place altars, while *ex-votos* were images of miraculous intercessions, each of which included the interceding sacred personage, the incident, and the date of intercession" (Giffords 2006, 197; see also Giffords 1992). These Mexican paintings follow a visual typology similar to Italian votives. Salvatori explains:

> The spatial configuration of Italian painted ex votos, often measuring twelve inches in height and twelve to twenty-four inches in width, marks two distinct and uneven parts: the smaller part, usually but not always the left upper corner, is dedicated to the heavenly figure or being, often floating on luminous clouds. The Madonna, Jesus, or a saint's gaze or outstretched hand occasionally reaches out to the supplicant, shortening "the invisible thread" between them. The rest of the space, the larger portion of the painting, is taken up by the human, and the visual representation of the miraculous event from domestic interior sickbed scenes of illness or recovery to outdoor natural weather disaster, household or work accidents or crime. At the bottom individualizing inscriptions: the

name of the supplicant, the date of the event, only occasionally the name of the painter; votive acronyms (*P.G.R*, Per Grazia Ricevuta [for grace received]; *E.V.*, Ex Voto; *V.F.G.R.*, Voto Fatto Grazia Ricevuta [vow completed for grace received]); and/or brief written accounts of the specific miracle, often misspelled and grammatically fractured. (Salvatori 2010, 29; see also Carroll 1992, 84)

All such paintings allow spaces for the communication of a supernatural narrative and, very significantly, a sense of perspective that allows the observer of that visual or verbal account to feel as if he or she is a member of an audience viewing the unfolding of an individualistic, private, miraculous human drama.[5]

Ex-voto as the Visualized Art of Supernatural Narrative

Christianity has played a tremendous influence on Western art, architecture, and crafts over the last 2,000 years. "Much of the history of Western art coincides with the history of the Christian Church, and much of its iconography depends on and derives from the specific events, doctrine, influential figures, devotional movements, and trends of the Roman Catholic Church" (Giorgi 2004, 6). Christian art in its most traditional sense has taken a variety of forms from sculpture and manuscripts to paintings and frescoes, from icons and fabrics to stained glass and ex-votos.

Ex-voto then is both a term in the history and spirituality of Christianity, particularly Roman Catholicism, as well as a term found in the study of the history of art, archaeology, folklore and folklife, and religious studies designating a particular type of religious and artistic expression: a piece of material culture produced in response to a vow made to a member of a sacred pantheon. Ex-votos intrinsically are not domestic religious material culture, but when expressed as paintings they often depict dramatic domestic situations. Votives are public religious objects that share a kinship with the experiential narratives that folklorists call *memorates* or private, first-person accounts of encountering the supernatural through miraculous events (Degh and Vazsonyi 1974); in this sense, ex-votos evoke that quality from the Middle Ages of being "speaking" gifts of thanks. If a memorate is generally understood as a first-person account of an experience with the supernatural, whether that be a ghost, demon, a god, or a saint, then an ex-voto is the objectification of that first-person encounter with the supernatural told as a visual narrative. Each ex-voto, therefore, is an individual object itself communicating a story about such direct interventions of God in the everyday life of the particular Christian believer. What the ex-voto does not communicate is a scene of an immediate actual apparition of the holy, even when a painted votive portrays the supplicant gazing ardently and directly up to a blessed figure hovering above the scene. This gaze represents prayerful vision as opposed to visual intercessory interaction.

This idea of objects and images associated with and relating narratives is intrinsic to the function of imagery in Christian art. Within institutional Catholicism, the potency and efficacy of religious imagery employed for didactic purposes can be observed historically in a letter of Pope Gregory the Great (590–604) to the iconoclastic Bishop Serenus of Marseille in which he reflects about the importance of images to teach the illiterate faithful about the Scriptures and generally to enable them to keep religious thoughts in their minds (Davis-Weyer 1986, 47–49). This function of images aided in the establishment of the practice of decorating and ornamenting Christian churches with visuals of the heavenly community for their beauty and for a pedagogical purpose. The usefulness of art developed in Western Christianity included the perspective that such imagery both taught the faithful about aspects of the tradition that they neither knew nor understood or read in all important Christian texts, while also reminding Christians about those aspects of faith that they had previously learned. In this sense, ex-votos also worked to instruct and remind the faithful about the very presence of Jesus, Mary, and Catholic saints in their lives. They were complements to the primacy of text with the supernatural reality of action that was the result of belief demonstrated through practice: the inclination to prayer and intercession.

Ex-votos took Christianity's developed love of the cult of the saints—a public cult—reinforced it as a private devotion, and then re-presented it as examples of performed belief and community public display events. As it emerged from the Middle Ages, "for the mass of its practitioners, Christianity became a visual and oral culture" (Webb 2009, 305), and ex-votos, as they developed, meshed seamlessly with such an apprehension of the tradition.

Ex-voto as Vow and Prayer

The appeal of ex-votos as objects of religious material culture is not limited to believers from particular social, economic, or educational ranks or levels of literacy. When reflecting on the influence of Christianity and its history on artistic representation, it is, of course, important to consider not only subject matter, features, and symbols emanating from the exclusive institutional life of the Church, its hierarchical functionaries, and secular governmental associates but also from the inclusive nonelite vernacular traditions of creative religious negotiation at the heart of the religious practice of all Christian believers themselves. The ex-voto is an exceptional expression of such creativity inspired by belief, vivifying the vernacular religious life of Christians. As acts of vernacular religion—that is, religion as it is lived, interpreted, negotiated, and created by individual believers (Primiano 1995, 37–56)—ex-voto offerings, and most certainly votive paintings, are in no way prescribed by the institutional Catholic Church. Votives are by their very nature multivocal. They are voluntary offerings and occasions for the creative expression and negotiation of the belief in the literal assistance of holy figures like the saints in everyday life and associated concepts such as heavenly intercession. Votives are representations of the religious aesthetic of believers integrated with the sensibilities of trained and untrained artists. Ex-votos are expressions of individual religiosity and, therefore, fall outside of the Catholic Church's theological perspective that one's spiritual relationship with God is best lived within the Christian community guided and *mediated* by the institutional Church. Individual religion has historically made the institutional Church uneasy because it eliminates this theologically and institutionally important principle of mediation. For this reason, ex-votos are rich examples of vernacular religion existing "apart from and alongside" (Yoder 2001, 80) the institution. In the case of ex-votos, object or painted, they are inspired by personal belief, created by artistic negotiators of the various traditions, and then assembled and housed around altars within the administrative normative framework of an institutionally sanctioned Church building.

The act of making a vow to God, that is, committing to the Deity to perform a particular action at a future time, is an important component of the prayer lives of many Christians. In Roman Catholic religious communities, individuals joined in fellowship make vows of poverty, chastity, and obedience as indications of their membership and commitment. Such "public vows" are legislated within the documents of particular religious orders of men and women, "recognized as public in Church law and are regulated not only by the law of a given religious community, but also by the general [Canon] law of the Church" (McBrien 1995, 1320). Institutional Catholicism supervises such vows and how they are observed in the course of everyday activities. These public vows are distinguished in the language of the Roman Catholic tradition from "private vows," which are "promises made to God singly and privately by individuals and [unlegislated] promises made within the context of a community" (McBrien 1995, 1320). The term *ex-voto*, a complex concept within Christian spirituality, relates to this ancient intimate Christian practice of "private" vow making to God, the Virgin Mary, or the saints proffered within a variety of contexts: from lengthy prayerful reflections to immediate moments of concern or even frightened exasperations. Within the history of Christianity, perhaps one of the more famous examples of spontaneous vow making can be found in the biography of the young, future Protestant reformer, Martin Luther, when in June 1505 the new law student was caught in a severe rainstorm. Almost struck by lightning and knocked to the ground, Luther's ardent religious response to this traumatic situation was to make a vow; he begged a saint to survive the furies of nature: "St. Anne, help! I will become a monk!" He petitioned the mother of the Virgin Mary, the patron saint of the miners of his youth. "Approximately two weeks later, in obedience to his vow, he entered the Augustinian monastery in Erfurt (Dillenberger 1962, xiv). The rest, as they say, is religious vow-making history.

For the American Roman Catholic practitioner, vow making as a part of asking divine intercession is certainly not an unusual practice. The physical action of the body to mark a prayer, prolong it, or thank or ask the divine for intercession has customarily been evidenced by entering a church and lighting what is called a "votive" candle—whether the illumination of a wax candle in a glass container among many other candles or the switching on of an electronic lightbulb (a mark of contemporary fire and insurance concerns and regulations). Here is mental prayer expressing a vow, wish, or desire embodied by the performance of a physical action. Calling up this tradition of candle lighting accompanying prayer, Michel Mollat du Jourdin, on the occasion of the American exhibition of a sample of mariners' votive offerings from the Montenero Sancutuary in North-Central Italy, reflects a European sensibility and expectation that ex-votos are a part of more commonly held knowledge, practice, or cultural recognition when he asks:

> Is it necessary to recall that an ex-voto offering is an object offered to God or to one of those, such as the saints, who can intercede with Him, and that its purpose is to express faith, and gratitude for a favour asked for and obtained? The ex-voto object, whatever it is, is also intended to express by its particular nature a commemoration of that especial act of grace, and to be the representative within the chosen sanctuary of the individual donor—and here we encounter a repetition of the universal symbol of the candle and the light it provides. (du Jourdin 1984, 11–12)

Ex-voto is a valuable dimension of how Catholics have actually prayed and an important element in understanding what is designated within Christian spirituality as "petitionary prayer." Margaret Dorgan notes in her discussion of prayer: "The basic sense of the word 'prayer' as entreaty, supplication, and petition is the introductory phase of approaching the One who is infinite power and limitless goodness. In addition to petition, prayer is also intercession, thanksgiving, repentance, adoration, and praise" (1995, 1037). Ex-votos, as expressive examples of devotionalism and vernacular religiosity no matter what the social station of the vow maker, can imply and include all of Dorgan's qualities of prayer.

The Collectible Sacred: Ex-votos in the Postmodern World

Having reviewed and explained the general history and definitional understanding of ex-votos, let us turn now toward more current developments in the cultural life of Catholic things. Such an endeavor is fruitfully enhanced with particular attention given to Italian painted ex-votos as viewed through the collection and practices of one individual—a methodology that folklorists and anthropologists use, as do other scholars of daily life, called "auto-ethnography" (Anderson 2006). I have been personally collecting ex-voto paintings since 2006 and offer here the lens of my auto-ethnography and personal narrative to explore this tradition. I use this method to address several key and compelling aspects of the ongoing ex-voto tradition. First, and more generally, my collection dovetails with the twenty-first century phenomenon of the digital collection of religious objects and as such is representative of the material practice of vernacular religion. Second, and more specifically, I speak reflexively about the very process of collecting: How I began my own collection of Italian ex-votos, especially Italian votive paintings, their sources, and the experience of collecting these objects via the Internet, and why their appeal remains powerful to me.[6]

Clara Bargellini in her catalog description of an enormous unsigned Mexican ex-voto oil painting on canvas (*Ex-Voto to the Virgin of the Rosary*), owned by the Wadsworth Athenaeum Museum of Art in Hartford, Connecticut, notes: "painted ex-votos are today usually thought of as small works by untrained artists, but some of the most important works in the history of art, including buildings and major paintings, have been created as acts of gratitude for miraculous interventions in human affairs" (2004, 43). Certainly, Titian's *Pietà*, ca. 1576, at the Venice Gallerie dell'Accademia, and Philippe de Champaigne's *Ex-Voto de 1662,* at the Musée du Louvre, are additional exemplars of ex-voto paintings by respected, formally trained, and identified artists.

My first encounters with the concept of ex-votos—as an action or object thanking the sacred forces following a promise made and a requested favor received—was not as either large or small painted forms. In fact, I had neither heard the term *ex-voto* nor knew of painted votives prior to taking an undergraduate "folk religion" course from American Folklife Studies scholar Don Yoder as a University of Pennsylvania undergraduate. Yoder loved to illustrate his lectures with slides, and I was immediately entranced by the anatomical figures and painted miraculous dramas that he used to illustrate relevant dimensions of both German and Austrian "folk" religion and religious folk art. I connected with Yoder's pedagogical point that a European sensibility to folklife studies could most certainly be applied to the study of the culture of everyday life in America. As I reflected on Yoder's lectures and applied them to my own experience of the culture of Catholicism, I realized that the concept of ex-voto was, in fact, familiar to me in countless expressions. I considered, for example, such forms as the novel, *The Song of Bernadette*, on the Marian apparition at Lourdes, France, by the Jewish writer Franz Werfel; the once-a-decade Passion Play performances at Obberamergau in Bavaria in southern Germany; the chapel and shrine to the Marian devotion, Our Lady of Perpetual Help, appended to Old St. Peter's Church above the shrine of St. John Neumann at Fifth Street and Girard Avenue in Philadelphia; and the

Lebanese-American comedian Danny Thomas's St. Jude Children's Research Hospital in Memphis, Tennessee.[7] All of these creations are the results of religious vows; they are all ex-votos: expressions of a promise made and fulfilled in architectural, literary, institutional, and dramatic form.

Yoder often spoke of his research trips to Europe and South America in his courses, and as I continued serving as his graduate student teaching assistant, I saw how he

some of the most important works in the history of art,

including buildings and major paintings,

have been created as acts of gratitude for miraculous interventions

complemented his time spent in archives and libraries in Austria, Germany, Italy, and Switzerland with excursions into antique shops, book dealers, and flea markets—as he did when at home—looking for religious ephemera and material culture. Yoder used his collection of American and European religious material culture, both Protestant and Catholic, in his teaching and research.[8] He paid especially close attention to the context of Pennsylvania German history and culture and its paintings; *fraktur* or illustrated manuscript art; medical, song, and ballad broadsides; political and military broadsides; sale bills; posters; house blessings and "letters from heaven"; and other forms of paper ephemera. Through his example, I decided to begin such an assemblage, but one that emphasized the culture of American and European Catholicism with as much devotion as Yoder had paid to European, and especially American, Protestant materials.

The major difficulty that I perceived in achieving my European collection goals through the 1980s and 1990s—beyond financing such an interest as a student and then a young professor—was that, other than traveling to Europe or elsewhere myself, I had no access to the European objects that I wished to collect. In addition, I knew few American dealers in Catholic material culture other than local retail Catholic religious goods stores (Primiano 1999), which were filled with inexpensive crafts and mass-produced Italian and Chinese-made import items. Those American sellers that I encountered asked such exorbitant prices for their objects that I grew frustrated at the possibility of ever finding such examples of objects from Europe or America. My first trip to Germany in 1989 did bring me to some antique shops near the great cathedrals in cities such as Munich where I saw eighteenth-century holy cards and sterling silver ex-voto body parts. Again, since I was still a graduate student with a modest income, I could not purchase such items, but I returned home resolved to continue collecting more modest American Catholic devotional artifacts, such as missals used to follow the order of the Latin Mass, holy cards, prints, etc., when I found them and to do so with greater attention. In the 1980s and 1990s, the preservation of such objects was only beginning (especially at the libraries and archives of such institutions as Boston College and Notre Dame), and they were not widely appreciated in America, often being disposed from people's homes or in the personal effects of deceased Catholic relatives.

Collecting American materials included American-made Catholic objects, but also European examples continuously transferred to North America—including French Canada—following the periods of European Catholic immigration. It was the small paper ephemera Catholic object known as the "holy card" that caught my initial enthusiastic attention because I already possessed a collection given to me by my grandmother (Primiano, in press(a)). My attraction to anatomical ex-voto forms was occasionally satisfied by folklorist colleagues purchasing examples for me in Europe, or even in Philadelphia. These were not silver antiques but newly molded tin examples. All such items were valuable to me because of their usefulness as illustrations in the classroom for my lectures on religious folklife. My searches led me to unexpected sources of supply: One of my favorite sites where I uncovered an astonishing cache of inexpensive Mexican votive paintings was, of all places, a Mexican restaurant supply warehouse in North Hollywood, California, where a literal heap of ex-voto *retablos* lay in a corner pile at very reasonable prices available for purchase along with the strings of molded red chile peppers and animal-form piñatas.

Other than such occasional examples from Latin America, however, I had no access to European votives, especially ex-voto paintings, which I had seen in abundance at religious folklife collections in 1989 in Germany (especially in the Rudolf Kriss Collection and the Gertrud Weinhold Collection, both owned by the Bavarian National Museum in Munich). Italian examples were simply not available to me. My interest in Italian "votive figures" as collectable items was further piqued by a 1989 *New York Times* "shopper's world" article written by a Rome resident. Louis Inturrisi offered an explanation concerning their availability at that time:

> Gradually the custom of purchasing ex-votos as thank-you offerings went out of fashion—
> due no doubt in some part to the temptation to thievery the silver figures afforded, but
> also due to their replacement with monetary donations. Where did all those ex-votos—
> the legs, hearts, heads, et cetera—that once shimmered on the walls of the great baroque
> churches in Rome and Naples go, once they were removed? Lately, they have been
> cropping up in antique stores in Italy and America and collectors have been combing flea
> markets in Rome and Naples to snatch up the best of what has become a new collectible.
> (Inturrisi 1989, Section 5, 12)

This article from the travel section included names of shops and flea markets in the Italian capital, as well as their locations for prospective collectors, mentioning that buyers also be aware of wooden "plaques in primary colors in a primitive style . . . that are harder to come by, but they are easy to carry." It was on a trip to Rome for the canonization of Philadelphia's Mother Katherine Drexel in 2000 that I purchased from an antique shop my first Italian ex-voto: a silver nineteenth-century heart (see figure 13).

I had to wait until I was introduced to eBay, the online auction and shopping website founded in 1995, to search and procure a variety of Catholic objects, eliminating the cost of travel and hotels as well as language barriers to ask questions such as dates of creation and even price. An examination of eBay's website reveals some remarkable numbers touted by the company: "With more than 94 million active users globally, eBay is the world's largest online marketplace, where practically anyone can buy and sell practically anything . . . eBay connects a diverse and passionate community of individual buyers and sellers, as well as small businesses. Their collective impact on e-commerce is staggering: In 2010, the total worth of goods sold on eBay was $62 billion—more than $2,000 *every second*" (eBay, "Who We Are").[9] As I became familiar with eBay's departments and procedures, I was soon astonished by the assortment of Catholiciana—the material world of Catholic culture and tradition—available for bid in this digital context. It has always seemed an ironic twist that for many decades Americans, in general, have raided the treasures, humble and grand, of Catholic Europe for, in the words of University of Chicago literary and critical theorist Bill Brown: "Just as the Old World has considered the New World a vast geographical field for imperial expansion, so the New World came to consider the Old a vast cultural field for expropriation" (Brown 2001a).

The variety of such items available for digital auction were undoubtedly assisted by the seismic institutional shifts and changes in Catholic devotionalism, spirituality, and ritual promulgated by the Second Vatican Council, the reforming meeting of the Roman Catholic Church (1962–1965) championed through the pontificates of Popes John XXIII and Paul VI. Beginning in the mid-1960s, clergy and laity began to discard traditional sacramental objects such as relics, Tridentine-style vestments, and saints' statues, since they no longer were seen as complementary to the *Novus Ordo*, or the revised form of the Roman Rite Mass, also called the Mass of Pope Paul VI, promulgated by the Council's liturgical reforms. Changes in personal attention to material objects of devotion in Catholic sanctuaries dovetailed with suggested transformations in personal devotions during Mass. During the liturgy, the congregants were now requested to participate in the ritual as a community. Mass was to be offered in the language of the local congregation for greater understanding and participation and no longer in ecclesiastical Latin. Personal devotions, such as the rosary, prayers on the back of holy cards or contained in prayer books, and missals—the hallmark of the liturgical experience of earlier generations of American Catholics attending Tridentine Masses (that is, the liturgy developed following the Catholic Reformation's reforming Council of Trent, 1545–1563)—were de-emphasized in what is now commonly referred to as the post–Vatican II period when the unifying Eucharistic life of the Church family was

Liturgical transformations, starting in the mid-1960s, caused changes to or the elimination of parish-sponsored saint and Marian devotions

stressed as the proper focus of worshipful attention. Catholic laity were challenged to be not merely ritual observers but ritual participants in the liturgy.

Liturgical transformations, starting in the mid-1960s, caused changes to or the elimination of parish-sponsored saint and Marian devotions, subsequently resulting in the release of many associated objects, such as relics or statuary, from Catholic sanctuaries (Dolan 1992, 429–30). Religious objects were then disposed of as trash or made available to the public in sales. Additional availability in North America and Europe of "vintage" (to use an eBay term) items of Catholic objects was caused by the closing of many Catholic churches in the post–Vatican II decades—especially in the larger cities—for lack of congregations; such closures came about for various reasons from changing urban–suburban Catholic demographics in America to loss of faith among congregations in Canada, Europe, and the United States. Shortages of priests to staff American parishes also necessitated their closing (see Roberts 2009; McBrien 2011). Even with the institutional Church being careful to provide its own newly built suburban parishes with architectural and devotional elements from older closed parishes—such as stained glass windows, statues, baptisteries, etc.—a veritable marketplace of Catholic sacramental items became available to those interested individuals—devotees, collectors, decorators, secularizers—who would seek them out. In the United States, the first decades of the new millennium saw another reason for church closings. It became necessary to sell off church properties and, therefore, transfer their contents to other local churches or even churches in other dioceses, to assist in the payment of financial settlements and legal fees resulting from lawsuits against the Church in cases of child sexual abuse by priests (Thavis 2011). An archdiocese such as Philadelphia would have a building filled with former sanctuary decorative ornaments and devotional objects for churches from across the country to take and reuse. Occasionally, these storehouses or even closed sanctuaries would have discretely announced sales of stained glass and other remaining items (see Campbell 2004).

A contemporary examination of the eBay website illustrates the remarkable amount of Catholic-themed material available as a result of the above causes and sources. Under the category of "Catholic Collectables," for example, there can be between 15,000 and 20,000 items available for inspection and bidding on any given day, a number that increases around the time of Christian holidays. This category includes: postcards, comics, lapel pins, key chains, and tobacciana (ashtrays, cigarette cases, lighters, etc., in this case with Catholic themes). It is under the "Religion and Spirituality" subcategory that one can locate previously used icons, prints, votives, relics, rosaries, holy cards, medals, statues, crucifixes and crosses, "bears and dolls," holy water fonts, stained glass, thuribles, tabernacles, monstrances, jewelry, charms, etc. eBay's website, in fact, includes what could best be described as a disclaimer to educate and assist those pursuers who lack clear knowledge about the Christian tradition: an institutional statement about the Catholic material that they carry or what an eBay representative referred to me as a "dictionary for sellers that gives meaning to what Catholicism and its related items are all about" (e-mail message to author, September 2, 2011). What is striking about this declaration is how lacking in nuance it is, misrepresenting Catholic history, sacramentality, practice, etc. with the oddest mélange of subjects and objects:

> There are different categories of Christians such as Protestants, Catholics, Greek orthodox, and Russian orthodox. Catholicism is generally associated with the religious beliefs, and practices of the Roman Catholic Church. The word *Catholic* is adopted from the Greek adjective *katholikos,* which literally means, 'general', 'universal'. It is most commonly used to refer to Christians in general as part of one church. The believers have accepted the pope who resides in the Vatican City, Rome, as the head of the church. There are various sacred objects that are connected to the practice of Catholic faith, such as vintage, relics, apparels that are used in the religious sacraments, and rituals. Believers in Christianity use common objects of faiths, which may include crucifix, scapular, chalice, etc. Many believers in this faith generally have 'Sacred Heart,' a framed picture of Jesus Christ, which they believe to be a source of protection. These objects of faith inspire them in their devotion to the lord and are also a source of positive energy. There are numerous collectibles available that the believers can own. Such pieces of faith objects includes the catholic dictionary, lamps, sacred heart badge 'Pieta' statue, scapular sets, old Catholic Encyclopedia book set, Archbishop Francis Spellman, statue of 'Kneeling Madonna and child Jesus', prayer book, statues of saints, and many other antiquities. One such antique object is the Holy Communion Charm catholic jewellery, which is made of 14k gold. These faith collectables and memorabilia help to create a sense of devotion. (eBay, "Catholic") (all spelling, punctuation, and style as they existed on the access date)

Again, this statement is highlighted by both an informality of style and a lack of precision in describing the Christian tradition and especially Catholic devotionalism. It can certainly be described as a vernacular religious description and assessment, and a rather remarkable example of the control eBay allows its own users to create explanatory text within the site itself.

Such an approach by the company is obviously quite appealing to its broad base of sellers. Indeed, through eBay, I located some excellent examples of American Catholic paper ephemera, and even Mexican *retablos*, but the closing month of 2006 was the first time that I actually encountered European ex-voto paintings on the site. The first source was an antiques dealer in Florida, and the second opportunity originated in Italy itself. Looking back on the experience now, it was as if a vortex had opened allowing me specifically to build a collection during a three-year period from 2006 to 2009. During this time, I had access to beautiful examples of what I felt were authentic older painted and silver votives being offered at auction. Most prominently, I relied on an American expatriate couple living in Italy who uncovered these pieces in various markets and antique shops as they traveled throughout the country, especially in Northern Italy. Posting their latest offerings of a dozen or more items, including many heart-shaped and painted ex-votos, they carefully personalized and described each item to the best of their ability, as can be seen in the following example:

> As we continue our travels around Italy searching for special treasures to bring you on Ebay, we are always looking for one of our particular favorites—the Italian Hand Painted Ex-Voto. We view them as one of the most beautiful and fascinating of the Italian Religious Art forms. Painted ex-votos have a long rich history here in Italy going back to the 15th Century.
>
> These painted images are offered to God, the Blessed Mother or a Saint as a form of prayer, and are created as a thank you for prayers answered. They tell a very personal story which is what makes them so interesting. They most often deal with illness, accidents and disasters. We are always captivated by the different artistic styles that have been created by the Artists from the various regions of Italy. . . . IN THIS AUCTION we are pleased to offer this wonderful Italian painted Ex-voto of a man seeking help for his cattle from Saint Chiaffredo, the Roman Soldier and Martyr. This enigmatic and devotional piece will hold a special place in your collection of antique religious artwork. . . .
>
> In case this is the first time you are checking with us, we are Americans currently living and traveling in Italy searching for unique items, which are designed and created here in Italy to present to you on Ebay. Please be sure to check out our other Auctions for Painted Ex-Votos, Hanging Sanctuary Lamp, Chalices, Incense Holder (Navicella), Ciborium, Statue Crown, Altar Vases (Portapalme), and a Wax Infant Jesus of Prague Statue, and many more treasures from Italy. (eBay 2008) (See figure 21)

As I began to win many of these ex-voto auctions, I grew to know these sellers via e-mail correspondence and inquired as to the sources of these pieces and their Italian region of origin. I also asked them repeatedly if they were certain of the authenticity of these votives, especially in light of the conspicuous contemporary production of fake *retablos* in the Mexican market crafted to resemble older paintings.[10] The couple assured me of the authenticity of the paintings based on location and context of discovery, as well as their own knowledge based on experience. I, and many other individuals, obviously believed their authentic provenance because at times the bidding for the especially unique votive paintings—which could cost as little as $300 or exceed $1,000—grew quite heated.

The 2008 economic downturn in the world economy played havoc on the amounts that eBay sellers could achieve in their auctions, and I began to win the auctions of the Italian ex-voto paintings at ever more reasonable prices (between $250 and $350). Soon, the couple e-mailed me that they had decided to give up selling on eBay for lack of sufficient profit. The final arrival of ex-voto paintings to me occurred in 2010 when on a trip to the United States the couple brought the last vestiges of their flea market searches to New York City and dropped them off to my colleague, folklorist Joseph Sciorra at the John D. Calandra Italian American Institute in New York City. Sadly, but providing an intriguing tinge of mystery, I never had the opportunity to meet or speak with my sources of this vernacular religious art. After 2010, my major contacts for Italian ex-votos were solely folk art dealers who occasionally would consign pieces from various collectors who contacted them. The appetite for things Catholic remains seemingly insatiable, but not even the resources of eBay sellers can continuously fulfill the desires of every collector.

Catholiciana Unmoored

The last twenty-five years have seen a growing interest by religion scholars in how believers and even at times nonbelievers encounter, understand, use, create, and re-create material culture to mark or imbue ecclesiastical and domestic spaces and places within their everyday religious lives with a sense of the sacred (for example, see McDannell 1995, 2004; Morgan 1998, 2005, 2007, 2010). Religious Studies, therefore, has joined Folklore and Folklife Studies in emphasizing the importance of such sacred materiality and how objects relate to the performance of religion (see Primiano, 1999; in press(b) for an extensive bibliography of folklorists studying religious material culture). David Morgan, whose work on the "material practice" of religious belief (2010) and the power of visual media to inform and help mold the sensibilities of religious Americans (2007) has led the field of American Religious Studies in important new directions, argues that "the study of the material cultures of religions is not the study of objects per se, nor a neurological approach to belief . . . . Instead the argument is that the study of religions will benefit from an approach that undertakes an abundant account of social life mediated in feelings, things, places, and performances . . . framed by the social construction of the sacred" (Morgan 2010, 12). Influenced by anthropologist Arjun Appadurai's discussion of the "social life of things" (1986), Morgan's 2007 text, *The Lure of Images*, is especially useful for its treatment of practices of consumerism, consumption, and display in America related to religious images. He offers a story about the use of non-

Catholic religious objects outside of their traditional religious context that is especially relevant to my discussion of the life of Catholic ex-votos, once they depart from their original shrine or church contexts. The case in point that he puts forth is the appropriation of the religious culture of Native Americans in the United States and its application to "New Age" religion, which fabricates its own mythology "as an avenue to lucrative non-Indian interest in self-help, therapeutic spirituality" (Morgan 2007, 248). Kachina dolls and sand paintings have been particularly popular as "mass-produced versions of authentic Indian artifacts . . . widely collected as *objets d'art*, as genuine artifacts, as high-grade simulacra, and as inexpensive tourists' souvenirs. In fact, many are made and sold by Native American artists or artisans, available on the internet no less than at reservations, national parks, and in tourist shops along interstate highways throughout the West and southwest" (Morgan 2007, 246–47). Morgan explains that Navajo weavers and sand image makers—upon realizing the interest of collectors and the opportunity to benefit financially—negotiated their own sanctification traditions. With regard to sand paintings, they deprived the images of "the right details" rendering them "impotent and safe for commodification and public display" (247–48). Such decisions about world religious objects used outside the context of their original religious purpose as *objets d'art* have wide implications when considering the life of Catholic ex-votos in the twenty-first century.

The commodification and consumption of religious images has certainly not been limited to Native Americans, as Roman Catholicism, the historic tradition of Western Europe, faces a similar state of affairs concerning its own myriad sacramental objects. Church and shrine stores; lay-owned religious goods shops (Primiano 1999)—whether specifically for Roman Catholic, New Age, Gothic, or African-based religions; secular establishments such as corporate book purveyors (for example, the now-defunct chain known as Border's Books); and the electronic convenience of eBay and other web-based outlets are expected and unexpected sites for the sale and purchase of Catholic religious objects in the twenty-first century. The variety of religious and secular sources of Catholic religious material culture of every sort in post–Vatican II and postmodern contexts have led to an abundance of objects unmoored from their ritual or sacramental foundations and re-presented as collectables and art. Religious objects, such as ex-voto paintings, thus, have taken a journey from materialization of memorate to biddable auction items on the international sacramental marketplace. Depending on the buyer and their understanding, appreciation, and faith, the Catholic objects sold by eBay in its electronic pages as well as these other outlets can be consumed with either a centuries-old appreciation as the sacramental presence of saintly holiness (see Peter Brown's *prasentia* of the sacred, 1981, 86–105) or in an ironic mode of incredulity in owning aspects of material belief still fostered and represented by what for some is a fading religious institution (see McDannell's Catholic kitsch, 1995, 163–97) or, perhaps, both attitudes balanced in the same individual.

The auctioning on eBay of particular items of Catholiciana has naturally been a source of concern for some Catholics. A writer for the Philadelphia archdiocesian weekly newspaper, *The Catholic Standard and Times*, opened her report (Brinkmann 2006) on the threat of a Catholic eBay boycott in 2006 due to the auctioning of relics with the following exclamation: "The flesh and bones of our canonized saints are being auctioned off to the highest bidder every day on the popular on-line auction site, eBay, and some Catholics think the only way to stop the practice is to boycott the site." In 2008, the sale of relics even received a negative reaction from Cardinal José Saraiva Martins, C.M.F., Vatican Prefect of the Congregation for the Causes of Saints, who vigorously castigated eBay for selling saints' relics as "totally unacceptable business" (Catholic News Agency 2008). eBay's response to such complaints has been to strengthen its policy toward trafficking in the human body. The statement, "Human Remains and Body Parts Policy," on the eBay site reads:

> We don't allow humans, the human body, or any human body parts or products to be listed on eBay, with two exceptions. Sellers can list items containing human scalp hair, and skulls and skeletons intended for medical use. . . . What are the guidelines? Items that contain human scalp hair (such as lockets or wigs); Clean, articulated (jointed), non-Native American skulls and skeletons used for medical research are allowed. If you are selling a first-class relic, you must state in the item description what the relic is made from. If it's a human remains it can't be sold if it's made from any body part except human scalp hair. What you cannot sell, according to eBay—even if the seller states that these items are used for medical research—are Native American grave-related items, including skulls and skeletons intended for medical research; Tibetan prayer skulls; organs; bones; blood; waste products; body fluids; sperm; eggs; any of these items included as a gift, prize or giveaway in connection with another item listed on eBay. (eBay, "Human Remains and Body Parts Policy") (all spelling, punctuation, and style as they existed on the access date)

eBay's policy aside, the site, of course, continues to auction the relics of Catholic saints and Christian martyrs, which to anyone familiar with the culture of Catholicism are obviously what the tradition has considered "first-class," that is, relics that are actual fragments, usually the bone, of a holy person. The irony of the reaction of some Catholics to this issue is that relics, of course, have been trafficked within the tradition since their recognition as important presences of the sacred within Latin Christianity in late antiquity (Geary 1991). Further, it is fascinating that there has been no outcry from the Church about other religious objects sold via eBay, given that the eventual purpose for all purchased items is ostensibly unknown, and possibly secularized. Ex-votos, in particular as vernacular religious material culture with a distinctively religious purpose, seemingly do not interest the institutional Church when used in a nondevotional way, for example, as Mexican restaurant decorations. Certainly, as any pilgrim to Vatican City's crowded, and at times raucous, religious goods shops can attest, the institutional Catholic Church cannot control what or how imagery and objects associated with the tradition are sold in its own shops, let alone how they might be used.

Religious objects certainly can take on lives of their own even after being discarded, sold, or possibly stolen from churches and holy places. Sociologist Michael P. Carroll indicates that, in the case of painted ex-votos, older examples in Italian sanctuaries

Ex-votos . . . as vernacular religious material culture . . .

seemingly do not interest the institutional Church

when used in a nondevotional way

"were routinely discarded to make room for new ex-voto," some were lost due to deterioration from lack of care, and many votives were stolen (1992, 84–85). Sociocultural anthropologist Allen F. Roberts, however, is not surprised that such objects have a life when separated from their original context, for as he clearly states: "Devotional images cannot sit still. . . . Religious . . . images float or seem to sometimes possess an uncanny ability to get up and go, drifting off in startling new directions to fulfill astounding new purposes. . . . Devotional images not only permit but provoke re-signification" (2010, 115, 132). It is the ambivalent nature of such images to sustain many "expressive journeys" of use and relevance into various religious traditions that makes them so powerful (2010, 122). Roberts specifically cites the use of chromolithographs—printed color images—in Haitian Vodou, a distinctive religion that is a hybridization of African religiosity and French Roman Catholicism, as one example of imagery translated to a new sacred space and made ready for new religious performances. Of course, here, though the traditional images of Catholic saints, Jesus, and the Virgin Mary in a variety of devotional forms are re-contextualized and shifted, there is a shared system of sacred meaning about the holy personages and their material visualization. There is also a shared tradition between Roman Catholics and Vodou practitioners concerning the affectionate domestic and ritual display of these sacred images. What about those commodified, commercial contexts when religious objects traverse boundaries unintended by those who originally created them, as well as the audience for which they were originally intended?

One example that comes to mind is the selling of Catholiciana in mass-market bookstore chains where I have observed Catholic plastic statues of the Virgin Mary and the Sacred Heart of Jesus made into banks and painted with loud colors and glitter. Who is the intended audience here, and which corporate executive thought it was appropriate to mass produce in China "Jesus Money Box Purple" for the American market? What sort of enterprising decorator decided in a book of interior design that displaying Mexican *retablo* paintings among other "tribal" arts was "a powerful source of inspiration" (Barnard 1998, 14) and, therefore, appropriate to be objectified along with so many other international forms of art, in this case as "charming hand-painted . . . local miracles" hung "above the cupboards" of an illustrative kitchen (Barnard 1998, 124, illustration)? In such commodification, the weight of the commercial enterprise prompts the conclusion that these devotional images have had the "holy" deconstructed right out of them. At least in the eBay universe, Catholic objects retain some value via their commodified descriptions as "vintage," "old," "antique," "rare," "unique," or "authentic."

The possibility of individuals standing in the presence of material dimensions of Catholicism that mark significant performative expressions of everyday life yet "gazing" upon them with a complete lack of appreciation or understanding, or even, perhaps, disdain for their cultural significance and for the people engaged with them, are responses that have been noted by folklorist Joseph Sciorra in his ethnographic work on the experiences of contemporary Italian-American Catholics. In what he describes as the "super-gentrification" that has transformed the physical, economic, and cultural landscapes of Williamsburg in Brooklyn, power relationships, local identity, and public life have been shifted and transformed as "bohemian hipsters"—seeking more affordable housing outside of Manhattan—have entered the once multiethnic, working-class neighborhood in greater numbers. The shift in power relations, Sciorra cites, is richly apparent when the Italian-American Catholics hold annual religious processions—a tradition since the 1880s—with their colorful statues of saints decorated with flowers being boosted into the air on the shoulders of festival workers and devotees and adorned with ribbons filled with cash votive offerings. In such instances, the images and their votive accompaniments are observed more like props in a filmed re-creation of a distant American world than a sincere display of public ethnic American Catholic religiosity: "The hipsters, for instance, have no desire to be part of the Catholic community—they snap photographs of processions like they were visiting Disneyland—and they equate the tradition of donating money during the processions with public panhandling" (*Center for 21st Century Studies* newsletter 2011, 4; see also Gonzalez 2010). There is little doubt that Catholic sacramental objects will continue to be bought, sold, traded, appreciated, stared at in disbelief, and disdained in the twenty-first century, in the same way that saints' relics were "translated" from place to place almost from the beginning of the Christian system of belief (see Brown 1981; Geary 1991).

Collecting . . . Yourself

In his provocative assessment of objects, collectors, and the act of collecting, cultural theorist Jean Baudrillard offers the notion that individuals have passion for "things," and that collectors are passionate for objects removed from their original functional contexts. For Baudrillard, object collection is itself a form of the expressive culture of the abstract self: "For what you really collect is always yourself" (2006, 97).[11] While I do not accept Baudrillard's neopsychoanalytic take on collecting as the "joy of possession" related to "a powerful anal-sadistic impulse" producing "the urge to sequester beauty" (55), I do see much of myself in the time and care and pride I take to locate and acquire Catholic ex-voto paintings—finding and owning these expressions of vernacular religion. Since I have directed the energies of my career to unlocking the mysteries of why people are religious in their everyday lives, it is not surprising that art visualizing the drama of desperate need, religious consolation, and miraculous intervention—expressed in a form accepted, but not prompted by, the institutional Church—would interest me. These paintings are the visualized expressions of vernacular religion and vernacular Catholicism in action, the unspeakable dramas of religious life shedding light on these otherwise muted mysteries.

One of the hallmarks of twentieth- and twenty-first-century scholarly work on material culture or the study of objects in everyday life in folklore, anthropology, archaeology, art history, classical studies, religious studies, literary criticism, critical theory, etc. has been to open the conversation to include not only how individuals make and influence the shape of things but also how things influence the shape of individuals (see, for example, Candlin and Guins 2009). Emerging from these studies of the production, distribution, and consumption of objects has been the reflection on the culture of collecting objects and the implications of the passionate collection of things by individuals.

As this essay reveals, the phenomenon of collecting religious "things" has a vital life of its own, mixing commercialism, art, curiosity, and faith. Bill Brown, the developer of the concept called "thing theory" (2001b) working on the "mania" of collecting in the United States (2001a, 2003), has mused that acts of collecting "generally depend on a form of consumption, but a form in which the product is carefully preserved, not used or used up; on the other hand, they are clearly acts of production, the making of the collection per se, the creation of a certain order" (Brown 2001a). It was my decision to "order" the ex-voto paintings in my collection by framing each of them in consultation with framer Art Forster of Wayne, Pennsylvania. We carefully examined each piece and decided on the style of frame, with certain paintings being grouped together for stylistic or aesthetic reasons by giving them the same frame. Given the pretensions of individuals critiquing folk art as aesthetically primitive, limited by its subject matter, and not as valuable and appealing monetarily, visually, or socially as so-called "fine" art paintings, I have made the decision to frame all vernacular religious art, especially ephemera and paintings, just as fine art is framed (see comments on the fate of New York City's American Folk Art Museum, Pogrebin, 2011). Since the object has already been plucked out of its original aesthetic, functional, performative, crafted human context of use and/or appreciation, I feel that by presenting these objects from everyday life as framed art their presentation can be used to teach viewers about how important, beautiful, and useful such objects were and are.[12] Furthermore, as I am especially interested in using these objects for classroom instruction, lectures, or exhibition, framing them strikes me as also the most practical, most protective, and most aesthetic approach.

One additional quality of my experience of ordering these votives purchased via eBay is worth noting. I have always been struck by the capacity of objects to generate narratives about their acquisition for later communication to family, friends, colleagues, students, and audiences. Such objects are reflectively ordered and framed in personal experience narratives that can become performative items in a collector's repertoire. Perhaps, this essay is a perfect example of just that creativity in written form, invoking folklorist Susan Stewart's thought that "the collector constructs a narrative of luck which replaces the narrative of production" (1993, 165). Because of my usual ability to recall where I purchased a particular object, in which setting, and the cost, I have found it unusual that my eBay auction purchases have not generated such specific tales or lasting memories for each of my ex-voto paintings. I suspect that it may have something to do with the significance of space and place in the experience of such procurement. As exciting as it can be at the moment of bidding in an eBay auction, it does not become a lasting memory. There is a blandness and sameness to the auction process, and even to the achievement of securing the object at hand. I, however, have very distinctive memories of the personal interactions involved with receiving gifts of Catholiciana from students, purchasing pieces of pottery, and procuring ex-votos directly from folk art dealers. As grateful as I am to eBay as a source for my collection, perhaps I am now working to detach and unmoor these Catholic objects as individual articulations of Catholic belief and practice from their digitally cold and unrelenting spring of mercantile captivity represented by the eBay experience.

What then will become of the resilient ex-voto? I find this question especially captivating considering that these objects of belief have endured and kept their place in succeeding cultures and religions for thousands of years. Georges Didi-Huberman's poetic essay on the ex-voto observes:

> Votive images . . . cut across time. They are common to highly disparate civilizations. They disregard the cleavage of paganism and Christianity. . . . Votive forms are capable of both

disappearing for a very long time and reappearing when one least expects it. They are just as capable of resisting any perceptible evolution. . . . They are not initially very easy to discern: the history of art ignores them and ethnology scarcely professes to analyse them formally. They are there, however, in us and around us, ghosts returning, surviving or living on. (2007, 7, 14)

Thus, the power of the ex-voto as a devotional object and image—whether a wax or silver piece of anatomy or a painted drama—endures in its meshing of the mundane and the sacred, in its compelling visuality, and in its humble beauty expressing the drama of the human experience.

ACKNOWLEDGMENTS

I wish to thank Joelle Collins, Ben Danner, Kathy McCrea, John DiMucci, Laura Sauer Palmer, Nicholas Rademacher, Lisa Ratmansky, Patti Stocker, William Westerman, as well as Sara Drew of Cabrini College's Holy Spirit Library for their assistance. I am especially grateful to Rosangela Briscese and Joseph Sciorra for their unfailing support, and to my colleague Nancy Watterson, who read final drafts of this article.

NOTES

1. See De Oliveira (2010, 20–25) for a presentation of vivid examples in Brazilian sanctuaries and Lettieri (1984, 47–55) for a discussion of an Italian context.

2. See Freedberg (1989, 136–37). The University of Pennsylvania Museum of Archaeology and Anthropology, for example, has several Etruscan terracotta votives in the form of heads and feet on display (see Turfa 2005, 45, 48–49). See also Turfa (1994) for a discussion about these objects and their role in Etruscan religious practice. Greek traditions in Paestum, a Greek colony in southern Italy, are referenced in Ammeiman (2002); see also Forsen (1996).

3. See, for example, the *Ecclesiastical History* of Christian bishop and historian Eusebius of Caesarea (ca. 260–ca. 339) (Eusebius 1984) who relates the story (Book 6, Chapter 5) of the Alexandrian martyr Potamiana, who promised the soldier Basilides after his respectful treatment of her on the way to her martyrdom that she would pray for him when she was with the Lord.

4. The website of the Museo del Paesaggio in Verbania, Italy, notes:
   Ex-votos can be classified as follows:
     Nonmaterial: legacies of goods or money, novenas, pilgrimages, fasts, etc.
     Material:
       Representational: three-dimensional reproductions of parts of the body, tools, buildings, etc; paintings, oleographs, photographs, etc.
       Symbolic: hearts, plaits, candles, etc.
       Circumstantial: objects having physical relevance to the event (crutches, weapons, etc.)
       Gifts: jewels, cloth, animals, etc.
       Buildings: churches, chapels, altars, etc. (Museo del Paesaggio 2011)

5. See Freedberg's discussion of the main figurative formulas of the votive genre as well as the popularity and effectiveness of the votive image (1989, 153–60).

6. For another collectors' statement about an assemblage of vernacular religious art, see Janis and Dennis Lyon's brief remarks (Carrillo and Steele 2007, 8)

7. Werfel's "personal preface" to what became a popular novel in 1941, and subsequently a 1943 film, states that he wrote the book in fulfillment of a vow—a sort of literary ex-voto—for escaping the encroaching Nazi occupation of France:

> In the last days of June 1940, in flight from our mortal enemies after the collapse of France, we reached the city of Lourdes . . . . It was, I repeat, a time of great dread. But it was also a time of great significance for me, for I became acquainted with the wondrous history of the girl Bernadette Soubirous and also with the wondrous facts concerning the healing of Lourdes. One day in my great distress I made a vow. I vowed that if I escaped from this desperate situation and reached the saving shores of America, I would put off all other tasks and sing, as best I could, the song of Bernadette. This book is the fulfillment of my vow. (1942, 6)

As noted, ex-votos can also take the form of buildings, and it was this manifestation that I encountered first in the United States. In Philadelphia, German-American parishioners of the Church of St. Peter the Apostle built a shrine to Our Lady of Perpetual Help over one hundred years ago as part of a vow made to safeguard the congregation from an influenza outbreak. Whether this narrative is factually true or not, this is the story that I was told as a child to great effect.

It is said that Thomas in periods of career desperation made a vow to St. Jude Thaddeus that if he achieved success, he would build a shrine to the saint in the United States. As one of the great American Catholic public votive actions of the late twentieth century, Thomas organized, helped construct, and contributed consistently to the hospital that opened in 1962 treating "catastrophic" children's diseases (see St. Jude Children's Research Hospital, 2011, and also the preface of Robert Orsi's (1996) study of devotion of St. Jude.

8. See, for example, illustrations in Yoder (2001; 2005) and throughout the journal he edited, *Pennsylvania Folklife*.

9. It was my friend, former Cabrini College Campus Minister, John DiMucci, who taught me how to query and use eBay for objects. My interest had been naturally piqued by gifts to me that John had won in the site's auctions.

10. See Roque and Schwartz (2004) for a discussion of contemporary Mexican *retablos*.

11. See also Stewart's discussion of collectors: "The ultimate term in the series that marks the collection is the 'self,' the articulation of the collector's own 'identity'" (1993, 162–63). A useful edited "collection" on the phenomenon of collecting for novice readers is Elsner and Cardinal (1994).

12. Folklorist Henry Glassie, writing about the importance of understanding "context" when approaching exhibitions of folk art, cautions that: "The danger is to think we are encountering folk art directly or interpreting it correctly when all we have done is to build a false context around it out of the culture we know best, our own" (1989, 17). Glassie writes about experiencing a collection of folk art through the perspective of its collector in his essay, "Folk Art in the Girard Collection" (1989, 16–24). The controversies over the dislocation of native, regional, vernacular, and folk art and artifacts in new contexts, especially in museum exhibitions, as well as the recontextualization of utilitarian objects for museum display, are discussed in Price (2001) and Karp and Lavine (1991).

WORKS CITED

Ammeiman, Rebecca Miller. 2002. *The Sanctuary of Santa Venera at Paestum II: The Votive Terracottas.* Ann Arbor, MI: University of Michigan Press.

Anderson, Leon. 2006. "Analytic Autoethnography." *Journal of Contemporary Ethnography* 35: 373–95.

Angenendt, Arnold. 2010. "Relics and Their Veneration." In *Treasures of Heaven: Saints, Relics, and Devotion in Medieval Europe,* edited by Martina Bagnoli, Holger A. Klein, C. Griffith Mann, and James Robinson, 19–28. New Haven, CT: Yale University Press.

Appadurai, Arjun, ed. 1986. *The Social Life of Things.* Cambridge, UK: Cambridge University Press.

The Bible. 1989. New Revised Standard Version. New York: HarperCollins.

Bargellini, Clara. 2004. "Ex-Voto to the Virgin of the Rosary." In *Painting a New World: Mexican Art and Life 1521–1821,* edited by Donna Pierce, Rogelio Ruiz Gomar, Clara Bargellini, 232–34. Austin: University of Texas Press.

Barnard, Nicholas. 1998. *Living with Folk Art.* New York: Thames and Hudson.

Baudrillard, Jean. 2006 [1968]. *The System of Objects.* New York: Verso.

Brinkmann, Susan. 2006. "Sacred Relics Sold on eBay: Boycott Urged." *The Catholic Standard and Times.* November 20. http://www.catholic.org/diocese/diocese_story.php?id=22071 (accessed September 19, 2011).

Brown, Bill. 2001a. "The Collecting Mania." *University of Chicago Magazine* 94(1). http://magazine.uchicago.edu/0110/features/mania.html (accessed September 25, 2011).

Brown, Bill. 2001b. "Thing Theory." *Critical Inquiry* 28(1): 1–22.

Brown, Bill. 2003. *A Sense of Things: The Object Matter of American Literature.* Chicago: University of Chicago Press.

Brown, Peter. 1981. *The Cult of the Saints: Its Rise and Function in Latin Christianity.* Chicago: University of Chicago Press.

Campbell, Dwayne. 2004. "Colorful Keepsakes from Closed Churches. A Sale Offers Pieces of Catholic History." *The Philadelphia Inquirer.* June 20. http://articles.philly.com/2004-06-20/news/25369459_1_windows-cost-stained-glass-windows-churches (accessed September 19, 2011).

Candlin, Fiona, and Raiford Guins, eds. 2009. *The Object Reader.* London: Routledge.

Carrillo, Charles M., and Thomas J. Steele. 2007. *A Century of Retablos: The Janis and Dennis Lyon Collection of New Mexican Santos, 1780–1880.* Phoenix: Phoenix Art Museum.

Carroll, Michael P. 1992. *Madonnas That Maim: Popular Catholicism in Italy Since the Fifteenth Century.* Baltimore: The Johns Hopkins University Press.

Catholic News Agency. 2008. "Sale of Relics 'Unacceptable Business,' says Vatican Cardinal." February 12. http://www.catholicnewsagency.com/news/sale_of_relics_unacceptable_business_says_vatican_cardinal/ (accessed September 19, 2011).

Center for 21st Century Studies, a Newsletter from the University of Wisconsin-Milwaukee. 2011. "Embodied Placemaking in Urban Public Spaces, Part 1." 1(Winter): 4–5.

Davis-Weyer, Caecilia. 1986. *Early Medieval Art, 300–1150.* Toronto: University of Toronto Press.

Degh, Linda, and Andrew Vazsonyi. 1974. "The Memorate and the Protomemorate." *Journal of American Folklore* 87: 225–39.

De Oliveira, José Cláudio Alves. 2010. "From Shape to Content: The Variety and Expression of Ex-votos in Brazil." *Requesting Miracles: Votive Offerings from Diverse Cultures* [exhibition catalog], 20–25. Winter Park, FL: Alice and William Jenkins Gallery at Crealdé School of Art.

Didi-Huberman, Georges. 2007. "Ex-Voto: Image, Organ, Time." *L'Esprit Créateur* 47(3): 7–16.

Dillenberger, John, ed. 1962. *Martin Luther: Selections from His Writings.* New York: Anchor Books.

Dolan, Jay P. 1992. *The American Catholic Experience: A History from Colonial Times to the Present.* Notre Dame, IN: University of Notre Dame Press.

Dorgan, Margaret. 1995. "Prayer." *The HarperCollins Encyclopedia of Catholicism,* edited by Richard McBrien, 1037–41. San Francisco: HarperSanFrancisco.

du Jourdin, Michel Mollat. 1984. "Preface." *Mariners' Votive Offerings in the Montenero Sanctuary/Ex voto marinari del Santuario di Montenero* [exhibition catalog], 11–14. Philadelphia: Port of History Museum at Penn's Landing.

eBay. "Catholic." http://popular.ebay.com/misc-c-d/catholic.htm?_sacat=914 (accessed September 2, 2011).

eBay. "Human Remains and Body Parts Policy." http://pages.ebay.com/help/policies/remains. html (accessed September 2, 2011).

eBay. 2008. Listing for "Italian Painted Ex-voto 'A Farmer Prays for His Cattle'" (Item number: 190259653408), October 16. [web page no longer available. URL unrecorded] (accessed October 26, 2008).

eBay. "Who We Are." http://www.ebayinc.com/who (accessed September 2, 2011).

Elsner, John, and Roger Cardinal. 1994. *The Cultures of Collecting.* London: Reaktion Books.

Eusebius. 1984. *The History of the Church from Christ to Constantine,* translated by G.A. Williamson. New York: Dorset Press.

Faeta, Francesco. 2007. "The Ritual Contexts of Italian Ex-Votos." In *Faith and Transformation: Votive Offerings and Amulets from the Alexander Girard Collection,* edited by Doris Francis, 60–61. Santa Fe: Museum of New Mexico Press.

Forsen, Björn. 1996. *Griechische Gliederweihungen. Eine Untersuchung zu ihrer Typologie und ihrer religions- und sozialgeschichtlichen Bedeutung.* Helsinki: Papers and Monographs of the Finnish Institute at Athens, vol. 4.

Francis, Doris, ed. 2007. *Faith and Transformation: Votive Offerings and Amulets from the Alexander Girard Collection.* Santa Fe: Museum of New Mexico Press.

Freedberg, David. 1989. *The Power of Images: Studies in the History and Theory of Response.* Chicago: University of Chicago Press.

Geary, Patrick J. 1991. *Furta Sacra: Thefts of Relics in the Central Middle Ages.* Princeton, NJ: Princeton University Press.

Giffords, Gloria Fraser. 1992. *Mexican Folk Retablos*, rev. ed. Albuquerque, NM: University of New Mexico Press.

Giffords, Gloria Fraser. 2006. "Promises and Answers: Retablos and Ex-Votos." In *Saints and Sinners: Mexican Devotional Art,* 197–99. Atglen, PA: Schiffer Publishing.

Giorgi, Rosa. 2004. *The History of the Church in Art*, translated by Brian Phillips. Los Angeles: J. Paul Getty Museum.

Glassie, Henry. 1989. *The Spirit of Folk Art: The Girard Collection at the Museum of International Folk Art.* New York: Abrams.

Gonzalez, David. 2010. "Still Taking to the Streets to Honor Their Saints." *New York Times.* June 6. http://www.nytimes.com/2010/06/07/nyregion/07feast.html (accessed August 28, 2011).

Inturrisi, Louis. 1989. "Votive Figures for Collectors." *New York Times.* February 19. http://www.nytimes.com/1989/02/19/travel/shopper-s-world-votive-figures-for-collectors.html?src=pm (accessed August 15, 2011).

Karp, Ivan, and Steven D. Lavine, eds. 1991. *Exhibiting Culture: The Poetics and Politics of Museum Display.* Washington, DC: Smithsonian Institute Press.

Lettieri, Federica Ugolini. 1984. "Historical and Artistic Considerations on the Collection of Mariners' Votive Offerings in the Montenero Sanctuary." *Mariners' Votive Offerings in the Montenero Sanctuary/Ex voto marinari del Santuario di Montenero* [exhibition catalog], 47–55. Philadelphia: Port of History Museum at Penn's Landing.

McBrien, Richard, ed. 1995. *The HarperCollins Encyclopedia of Catholicism.* San Francisco: HarperSanFrancisco.

McBrien, Richard. 2011. "Parish Mergers: So Tough to Balance Resources and Personnel." *National Catholic Reporter.* March 21. http://ncronline.org/blogs/essays-theology/parish-mergers-so-tough-balance-resources-and-personnel (accessed August 15, 2011).

McDannell, Colleen. 1995. *Material Christianity: Religion and Popular Culture in America.* New Haven, CT: Yale University Press.

McDannell, Colleen. 2004. *Picturing Faith: Photography and the Great Depression.* New Haven, CT: Yale University Press.

Morgan, David. 1998. *Visual Piety: A History and Theory of Popular Religious Images.* Berkeley: University of California Press.

Morgan, David. 2005. *The Sacred Gaze: Religious Visual Culture in Theory and Practice.* Berkeley: University of California Press.

Morgan, David. 2007. *The Lure of Images: A History of Religion and Visual Media in America.* London: Routledge.

Morgan, David. 2008. *The Sacred Heart of Jesus: The Visual Evolution of a Devotion.* Amsterdam: Amsterdam University Press.

Morgan, David, ed. 2010. *Religion and Material Culture: The Matter of Belief.* New York: Routledge.

Museo del Paesaggio. 2011. "The Collection of Ex-voto Paintings." http://www. museodelpaesaggio.it/en-en/home/collections/popular_devotion_section/the_collection_ of_ex_voto_paintings (accessed September 26, 2011).

Nolan, Mary Lee, and Sidney Nolan. 1989. *Christian Pilgrimage in Modern Western Europe.* Chapel Hill, NC: University of North Carolina Press.

Nystrom, Bradley P., and David P. Nystrom. 2004. *The History of Christianity: An Introduction.* New York: McGraw-Hill.

Orsi, Robert A. 1996. *Thank You, St. Jude: Women's Devotion to the Patron Saint of Hopeless Causes.* New Haven, CT: Yale University Press.

Pogrebin, Robin. 2011. "Options Dim for Museum of Folk Art." *New York Times*, August 24. http://www.nytimes.com/2011/08/25/arts/design/american-folk-art-museum-weighs-survival-strategies.html?pagewanted=all (accessed September 3, 2011).

Price, Sally. 2001. *Primitive Art in Civilized Places*, 2nd ed. Chicago: University of Chicago Press.

Primiano, Leonard Norman. 1995. "Vernacular Religion and the Search for Method in Religious Folklife." *Western Folklore* 54: 37–56.

Primiano, Leonard Norman. 1999. "Post-Modern Sites of Catholic Sacred Materiality." In *Perspectives on American Religion and Culture,* edited by Peter W. Williams, 187–202. Malden, MA: Basil Blackwell.

Primiano, Leonard Norman. In press(a). "Artifacts of Belief: Catholic Holy Cards in American Culture." In *Ephemera Across the Atlantic: Popular Print Culture in Two Worlds,* edited by Don Yoder. University Park, PA: Pennsylvania State University Press.

Primiano, Leonard Norman. In press(b). "Material Culture." In *Encyclopedia of Global Religion,* edited by W. C. Roof and M. Juergensmeyer. Thousand Oaks, CA: Sage Publications.

Roberts, Allen F. 2010. "Tempering 'the Tyranny of Already' Re-signification and the Migration of Images." In *Religion and Material Culture: The Matter of Belief,* edited by David Morgan, 115–134. New York: Routledge.

Roberts, Tom. 2009. "Parish Closing Traumas Spread." *National Catholic Reporter,* January 23. http://ncronline.org/node/3090 (accessed July 12, 2011).

Roque, Alfredo Vilchis, and Pierre Schwartz. 2004. *Infinitas Gracias: Contemporary Mexican Votive Painting.* San Francisco: Seuil Chronicle.

Salvatori, Mariolina Rizzi. 2010. "Understanding Ex-Votos." *Requesting Miracles: Votive Offerings from Diverse Cultures* [exhibition catalog], 28–35. Winter Park, FL: Alice and William Jenkins Gallery at Crealdé School of Art.

Stewart, Susan. 1993. *On Longing: Narratives of the Miniature, the Gigantic, the Souvenir, the Collection.* Durham, NC: Duke University Press.

St. Jude Children's Research Hospital. 2011. "All About Danny Thomas." http://www.stjude.org/stjude/v/index.jsp?vgnextoid=3f08fa2454e70110VgnVCM1000001e0215acRCRD&vg (accessed September 26, 2011).

Thavis, John. 2011. "Vatican Prepares Document on Clergy-Laity Relationship." *National Catholic Reporter*, June 28. http://ncronline.org/news/vatican/vatican-prepares-document-clergy-laity-relationship (accessed September 5, 2011).

Turfa, Jean. 1994. "Anatomical Votives and Italian Medical Traditions." In *Murlo and the Etruscans. Art and Society in Ancient Etruria*, edited by R. D. De Puma and J. P. Small, 224–40. Madison, WI: University of Wisconsin Press.

Turfa, Jean MacIntosh. 2005. *Catalogue of the Etruscan Gallery of the University of Pennsylvania Museum of Archaeology and Anthropology.* Philadelphia: University of Pennsylvania Museum of Archaeology and Anthropology.

Webb, Diana. 2009. "Domestic Religion." In *Medieval Christianity: A People's History of Christianity,* Vol. 4, edited by Daniel E. Bornstein, 303–328. Minneapolis: Fortress Press.

Werfel, Franz. 1942. *The Song of Bernadette,* translated by Ludwig Lewisohn. New York: The Viking Press.

Yoder, Don. 2001. "Toward a Definition of Folk Religion." In *Discovering American Folklife: Essays on Folk Culture and the Pennsylvania Dutch.* Mechanicsburg, PA: Stackpole Books.

Yoder, Don. 2005. *The Pennsylvania German Broadside: A History and Guide.* Philadelphia: University of Pennsylvania Press.

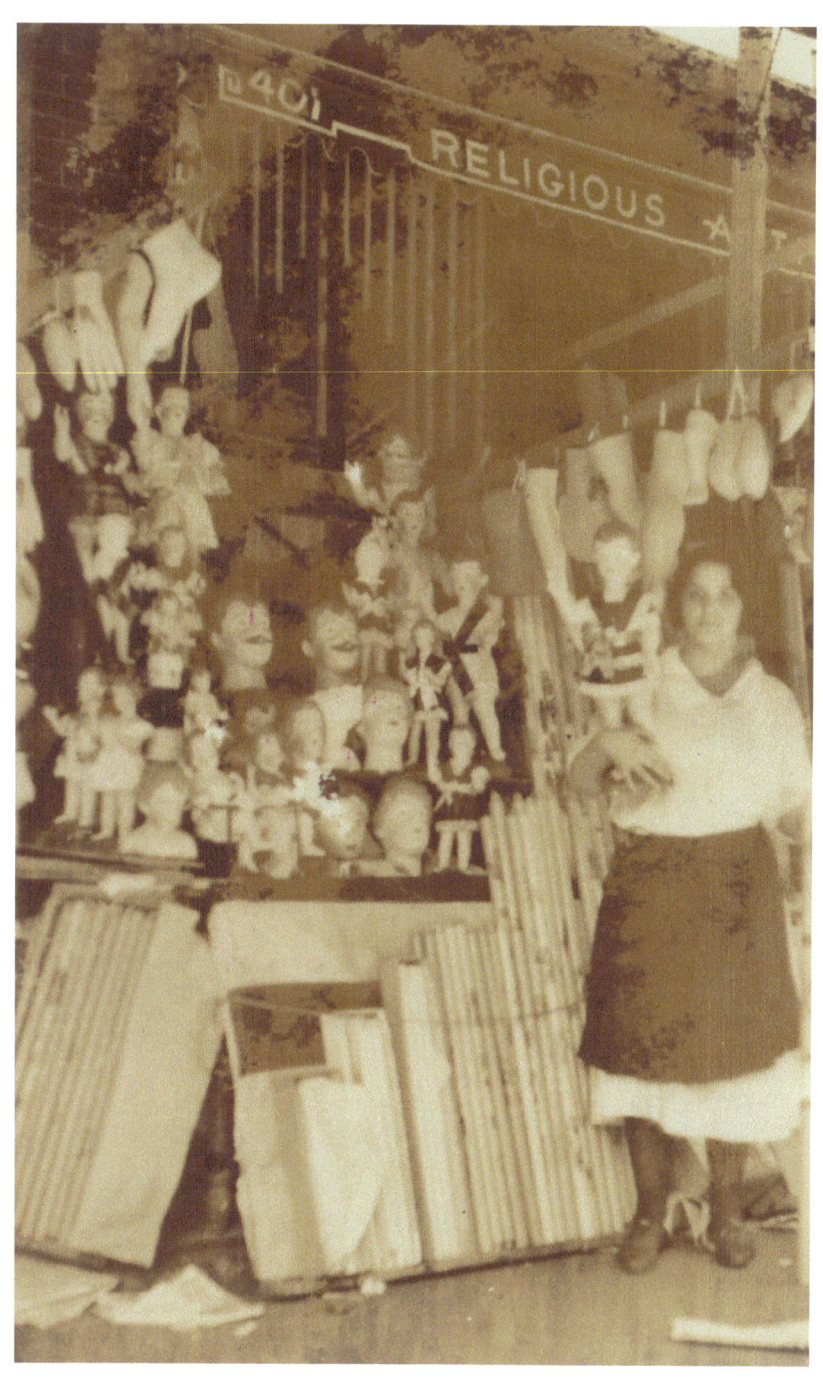

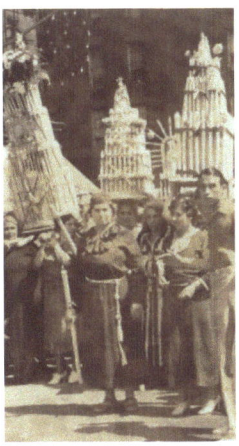

Miracles in a Land of Promise

Transmigratory Experiences and Italian-American Ex-votos

JOSEPH SCIORRA

IT WAS A MIRACLE that they left, that they extricated themselves from the forces that conspired to keep them in penury and subjugation. It was a miracle that they arrived, enduring oceanic journeys from village to metropolis outsmarting thieves and *padroni* along the way. It was a miracle that they survived, that they found work and shelter, that they fed their children and remained healthy. In achieving all this—and oh, how many were maimed, driven insane, jailed, or killed?—Italian immigrants of the Great Wave relied on their wits, their fortitude, and their resolve. And they also depended on the graces of the Blessed Virgin and the pantheon of Catholic saints who they ardently petitioned in their darkest moments of despair.

The Italian laboring poor brought to the United States their profound belief in the efficacy of prayer as well as the artistry to make visible their gratitude for heavenly intercession. The reciprocal system linking heaven and earth in thaumaturgy and votive offerings is a basic tenet of Roman Catholicism that takes many forms, from everyday objects, such as a healed child's dress, a pair of crutches, or jewelry, to acts such as walking barefoot in a procession or dressing a child in the facsimile of a canonized monk's robes (see Rossi 1986, 130–35). In the United States, Italian-American Catholics crafted, purchased, and displayed wax anatomical sculptures and pyramidal structures of candles and ribbons as offerings of indebtedness. Historian Robert Orsi's work on the Our Lady of Mt. Carmel *festa* in East Harlem, Manhattan, has done much to elucidate the religious and cultural context in which Italian immigrants created, used, and imagined votive objects and behaviors in the enactment of a family or "domus-centered bond" with the supernatural as part of an indigenous "theology of the streets" (Orsi 1985, 225). What we lack from an Italian-American perspective, however, is an understanding of the material aspects of the ex-voto itself and the processes by which "experiencing the physical dimension of religion helps *bring about*

Opposite

Wax votive figures and candles for sale during the feast of Our Lady of Mt. Carmel, Harlem, Manhattan, July 1924.

©Milstein Division of United States History, Local History & Genealogy, The New York Public Library, Astor, Lenox and Tilden Foundations.

Above

Detail, see photo page 45.

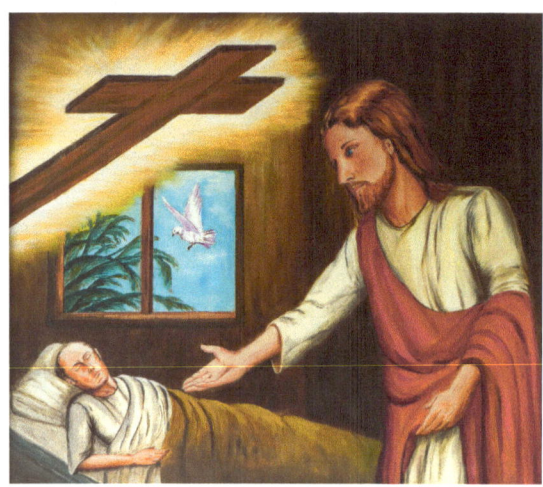

Voto
Natale Rotondi
1972, oil on canvas, 24 x 28 inches
Photo: Luca Fantini

religious values, norms, behaviors, and attitudes" (McDannell 1995, 2; see also Morgan 1998). Perhaps such a historical study is no longer possible, given the scant documentation of ex-voto makers or the economics of such ephemera deemed inferior, embarrassing, and "pagan" by the various powers that be. Today, we are able to converse with those Italian-American Catholics who continue to craft and exhibit a diversity of votive objects—from domestic altars to yard shrines—that emerge from both the intimacies of family traditions and studied revivalist interventions. The history of this Italian-American religious art has not been properly documented in any coherent fashion, a paucity this article seeks to rectify if only as prefatory for a future in-depth study.[1]

The *tavoletta votiva* (votive panel)—the small painting illustrating the moment of crisis for which a miracle is sought—does not appear to have existed in the United States.[2] Yet more research needs to be carried out before making such a definitive statement. Take, for example, the case of Natale Rotondi (1924–2009) of Bensonhurst, Brooklyn. Rotondi, a lathe machinist who emigrated from Mola di Bari (Bari province), Apulia, in 1952, learned to paint through a correspondence course in 1967–1968, and his representational oil paintings of still life and landscapes, often with Italian themes, were sought after by his relatives, neighbors, and *paesani* (Dossena 1995, 6–8). Knowledgeable of the *tavoletta* tradition from examples he had seen at the sanctuary for the Madonna of the Rosary in Pompei outside of Naples, among other places, Rotondi completed an ex-voto painting in April 1974 after surviving a bout with cancer. Instead of offering the work to a church, as is common, he hung it in the inner sanctum of the master bedroom he shared with his wife Isabella. When I interviewed him thirteen years later about his life and oeuvre, he interpreted the artistic elements and personal meaning of this votive work:

> And I prayed and I said, "If I get out of this wood, I've got to create a voto. *Fare un voto.* I've got to create a painting for myself." And so when I got better, then I began to paint this, which depicts a dying man; let's just say, he's just about to die. And the cross appears in the sky. The cross represents all the things that we have to endure on earth—all the troubles, the sorrows, the pain—all of this is the cross. That which we always shoulder for whatever happens, is the cross; we are condemned to carry it all our lives.

> And then, the dove of peace, which, if I was to die, there would be peace. The dove, you see, brings, ah, enters through the window and as it enters, the clouds dissipate, becoming

serene, that is, the invalid is healed, he's better. And all because the Lord arrived and said, "Arise." You understand? So in other words it's a composition, it's not a dream, it's nothing, I mean [not that] it's nothing, it's a room where these things emerge which in reality doesn't exist, but it exists as a fantasy, in my vision of things.

[. . .]

People wanted to buy it. It's not for sale. It's not for sale. It's mine. I keep it in the bedroom.

JS: It's beautiful.

It represents a lot for me. Let's just say, it's everything. Each person can judge [it] as they like, but for me it represents a story. It's my story. (interview with the author, August 7, 1985)[3]

Is it possible that Rotondi's *tavoletta votiva* is the only Italian-American example? While a methodical search has yet to be conducted, immigrant votive paintings are best sought not in the United States but in churches in Italy where they exist as artifacts of a transmigratory nature.[4]

Tavolette chronicling the emigration experience in their uniquely dramatic fashion have been reproduced in various publications, in particular those concerning the 26 million Italians who migrated worldwide over the course of a century.[5] Jorge Durant and Douglas Massy in their work on votive *retablo* paintings concerning Mexican migration, *Miracles on the Border*, offer a fruitful perspective for looking at the comparable vibrant Italian tradition of ex-voto paintings as they pertain specifically to the diaspora. "Simple, evocative depictions of the dangers and joys of life in the United States and the paradoxes and problems of international movement provide a compelling entrée to this votive art" (1995, 3), an assessment true for both Mexican *retablos* and Italian *tavolette*.

The earliest known migration-themed *tavoletta* I have located dates to the early nineteenth century. The Pia family—who emigrated to New York City where they eventually established a toy factory—commissioned the painting in 1805 and placed it in a church in the hamlet Piana di Forno, in the town of Valstrona (Verbano-Cusio-Ossola province), Piedmont (*IMAGES* 1986, 39). In the bottom half of the picture eight men, some with arms raised in supplication, stand in a sailboat cast amid a dark, churning sea. Seven names are listed in a scroll at the upper left: Gio' Batta Sesiani, Gio' Batta Tambornino, Gio' Tonolo, Gio' Peretti, Francecho Peretti, Giulielmo Zampone, and Annto Tonolo. Centered in the painting's upper space is a seated figure of Our Lady of Sorrows, seven daggers piercing her chest, with the dead Christ prone in her lap. To the Pietà's right, a *putto* holds a scroll with the inscription "G: R:" (*grazia ricevuta*, grace received).

Maritime *tavolette* from the era of steamship travel record nautical disasters during the Great Wave of Italian migration.[6] Antonino Carlo di Magnano and Giovanni [middle name indecipherable] Zabetta both gave thanks to the Black Madonna of Oropa from Biella, in Piedmont, for surviving a shipwreck on December 25, 1898, and July 4, 1903, respectively (Bevilacqua, De Clementi, and Franzina, 2002).[7] In the latter painting, the Statue of Liberty can be seen in the distant horizon.

Calamities compounded in the New World, as did miracles. On February 9, 1892, Luigi Caranta, from a Piedmontese mountain town, beseeched St. Bernard of Menthon (also known as St. Bernard of Aosta) to rescue him from a mine collapse (Agosti 1979, figure 32). The painting was donated to what appears to be the St. Bernard Chapel in the hamlet Desertetto in Valdieri (Cuneo province), Piedmont.[8] The scene depicts two men—one with arms raised—standing inside a cave with rubble outside the opening, and the saint—dressed in clerical robes and gripping the collared Devil chained by his side—gesturing toward the men from an aureola in the upper left-hand corner. The inscription in the lower left reads in part, "G. R. in America." Grace received in America.[9]

A *tavoletta* was donated to the Sanctuary of the Madonna of the Arch in

The Italian laboring poor brought to the United States their profound belief in the efficacy of prayer as well as the artistry to make visible their gratitude for heavenly intercession.

Sant'Anastasia (Naples province), Campania, illustrating a scene said to have taken place ("*successo*") in "New York" in 1909 (Rak and Giardino 1987, 142). The watercolor on paper (which was in turn glued to canvas) is of a snow-covered rural landscape with two wooden buildings in the foreground flanking a road running up the center to woods in the background. A dozen men are depicted. One man bludgeons (knifes?) another, while a second man, assisted by two policemen, lies bleeding on the ground. A third runs away down the road. Hovering in the sky are the icon of the dark-skinned Madonna of the Arch and Child on the left and St. Joseph and Child on the right.

Many immigrants without means succumbed to illness in a time of inadequate medical care. Anna Cavaleris née Grosso, "living in America" ("*residente in America*"), turned to Our Lady of the Flowers when she fell ill and, after receiving the grace on March 19, 1892, commissioned a painted ex-voto in thanks (Bevilacqua, De Clementi, and Franzina 2002). The *tavoletta*, placed in the sanctuary to the Madonna in Bra (Cuneo province), Piedmont, shows a woman in nightclothes propped up in bed, while a mustached man in a suit stands at the foot of the bed with his hands folded in prayer. The couple directs its gaze toward the Virgin standing amid a circular cloud formation in the painting's upper center.

In North America Italian Americans did continue the ancient practice of leaving inscribed plaques and tablets in thanks for divine intervention. Devotees of Our Lady of Mount Carmel thronged the sanctuary church on East 115th Street in East Harlem for the July 16th feast day, offering "gold and silver colored plaques," among other objects, in gratitude (*The Italians of New York* 1938, 89). Italian Americans from upstate New York journeyed to the Canadian pilgrimage site St. Joseph's Oratory of Mount Royal, Montreal, where they had marble plaques made. One such tablet reads:

TO DEAR

SAINT JOSEPH

SINCERE THANKS

THOS J. RUGGIERO, UTICA N.Y. 1954

These votive inscriptions were left in a chapel constructed in the first decade of the twentieth century by Brother André Bessette, a member of the Congregation of Holy Cross who was canonized in 2010.

In the United States, Italian immigrants and their descendants most often used wax, not metal, anatomical ex-votos as an expression of their heartfelt thanks. Orsi briefly describes an interwar scene from the *festa* held in honor of Our Lady of Mount Carmel in East Harlem:

> Vendors of religious articles set up booths along the sidewalks, competing for business with the thriving local trade in religious goods. The booths were filled with wax replicas of internal human organs and with models of human limbs and heads. Someone who had been healed—or hoped to be healed—by the Madonna of headaches or arthritis would carry wax models of the afflicted limbs or head, painted to make them look realistic, in the big procession. The devout could also buy little wax statues of infants. (1985, 3)

Photographic evidence indicates that these objects were mold formed, three dimensional, and usually painted. Devotees embraced these objects as they walked in the procession through the neighborhood streets, thus giving public testimony to the power of the supernatural in an individual's everyday life. The objects would then be placed

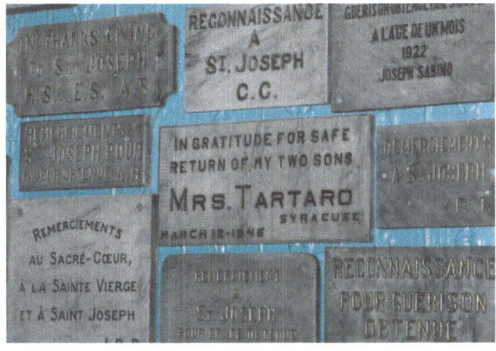

Marble votive plaques, St. Joseph's Oratory of Mount Royal, Montreal, August 2004.

Photo: Joseph Sciorra.

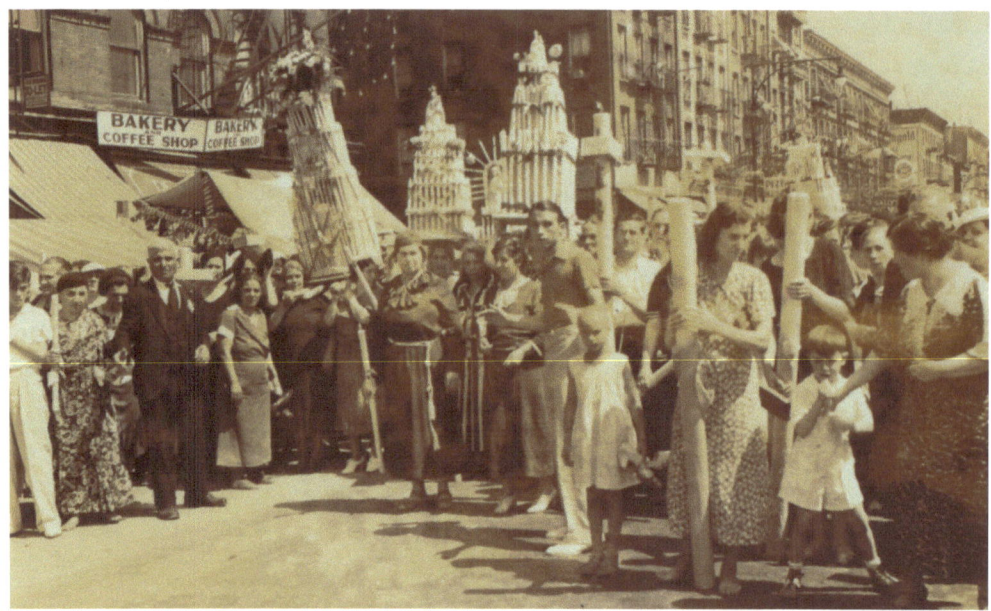

Carrying votive *cinti* and candles in the procession for Our Lady of
Mount Carmel, Harlem, Manhattan, July 1936.

©Milstein Division of United States History, Local History & Genealogy, The New York Public
Library, Astor, Lenox and Tilden Foundations.

as offerings on the altar where the particular statue of the feted Madonna or saint was
ensconced, be it a Catholic church, the storefront headquarters of a lay religious organization (Sciorra 2004, 16), or a temporary outdoor *festa* chapel. It is this very ceremonial promulgation that helped invest the object with efficacy and imbued it with
an authoritative aura of affecting presence (Freedberg 1989, 153–55; Armstrong 1981).
We can surmise that deposited wax ex-votos were eventually recycled, that is melted
down, and recast.

The mainstream, English-language press was fascinated with these anatomical reproductions and featured them in its coverage of Italian Americans. In 1906, an un-
identified *New York Times* reporter described the five-story *festa* chapel erected by the
members of the lay Society of San Rocco on Mott Street in Manhattan:

> Legs, arms, parts of the torso, faces, and such things in wax made a heaping of sacrifices
> to the saint. Some of the waxen figures were not attractive, but others were of the heads
> of children, skillfully molded and fashioned after the figures of Raphael's cherubs, which
> smile from the lower edge of his canvas in the famous Sistine Madonna. ("San Rocco
> Honored by Rival Factions" 1906, 7)

Thirty-one years later, *LIFE* magazine dedicated a two-page feature to another feast
in honor of St. Roch held at what is clearly St. Joachim's Church on the now defunct

Roosevelt Street.[10] Five of the ten photographs show rows of wax ex-votos or devotees transporting them. One caption informs the magazine's readers that "many of the priests regard such offerings as semipagan but do not forbid them" ("'Little Italy' Cloaks Its Healing Saint in Dollars" 1937, 71–72).

According to Stephen La Rocca, the current president of the St. Rocco Society of Potenza (founded in 1889), these very objects continued to exist up until the early 1980s, in the basement of St. Joseph's Church on Catherine Street, Manhattan, transferred from the razed St. Joachim's Church. The society resorted to renting the objects to procession marchers who were no longer able to readily buy the wax body parts from religious artifact purveyors. According to the "Financial Statement" dated August 16, 1982, the society collected $31 for such services that year. Soon afterwards, the church pastor at the time, according to La Rocca, "felt that they were pagan and unnecessary and stupid and 'Why do you need them?' and threw them away" (interview with the author, May 31, 2011). Since becoming president in 1990, La Rocca has helped reinvigorate lower Manhattan's public celebration for St. Roch, re-introducing the use of wax ex-votos imported from Calabria in 2006 (St. Rocco Society of Potenza):

> These signs and symbols are so strong in our, I don't want to say, in our genetic memory, maybe that's foolish, but our cultural memory, they are so strong. And they really fit a human need throughout the centuries, from before the birth of Christ, they meant something. So why all of sudden should they just die? Well, because the world's different . . . but to me there's a human need that's satisfied in there and I want to reintroduce this to our people. [. . .] Our world that we cherish so much is either going to be lost or has to be preserved. And it can't be preserved like a museum because if it's preserved like a museum it's forgotten. It has to be lived. [. . .] I think spiritually it's important and culturally it's important. We need to maintain this. [. . .] I want it to be there if somebody wants it. I don't care if they don't want it, and if they reject it that's ok. But I want it to be there if they want it. (La Rocca, interview with the author, May 31, 2011)

Thus reintroduced, these synecdochic portraits of the sick/healed individual (Didi-Huberman 2007, 10–14; Freedberg 1989, 156–60) provide insight into the mechanisms by which contemporary American Catholics invest religious meaning by renegotiating pre–Vatican II practices in the twentieth-first century.

Wax candles were historically used for another artistic votive object known as *il cinto*. Anthropologist Annabella Rossi's study of southern Italian religious feasts of the 1960s indicates the prevalence of these objects in the regions of Basilicata and Campania (1986, 71, 78).[11] Sometimes referred to as *la centa* in dialect and a "candle house" in English, *il cinto* (literally, truss) is a multitiered structure created with a circular, oval, square, or rectangular base. Unlit candles surround the armature and the construction is festooned with flowers, ribbons, and religious imagery. Crowning this votive structure is a statue or printed image of the feted saint or Madonna. Artisans were

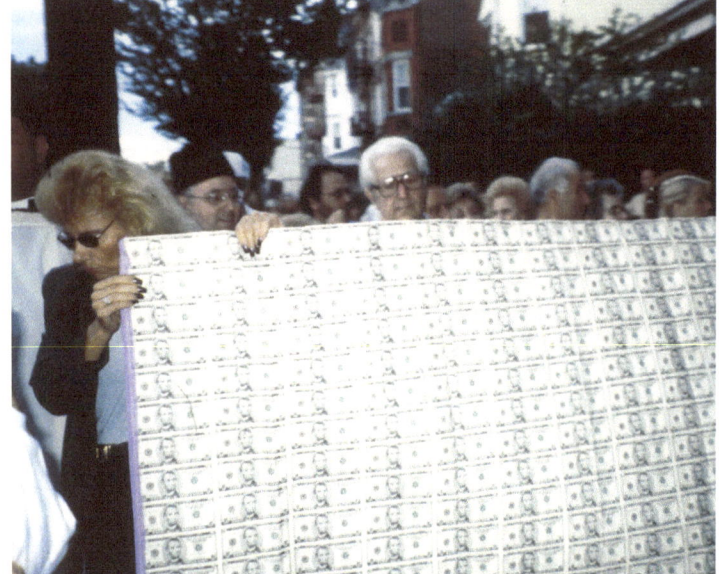

Presenting a votive "blanket" during the St. Gerard procession. Newark, New Jersey, October 1999.

Photo: Peter Savastano

commissioned to create *i cinti* both in Italy and the United States. A single individual, usually a woman, carried the structure on her head, or a small group transported it on a litter. This Italian-American practice continues in Melrose Park, Illinois, and Hazelton, Pennsylvania, where candle houses are considered "key ingredients" and part of the "language" of what constitutes a traditional religious *festa* (Rubino 1992, 37; 1987, 3, 14).[12]

Unique votive offerings are the ornamented and highly ordered "blankets" and "capes" of money created in honor of St. Gerard Maiella at St. Lucy's Church in Newark, New Jersey. Anthropologist Peter Savastano briefly describes these votive objects in his ethnography of the contemporary feast complex. The blankets are crafted at home and can take up to three months to complete (Savastano 2002, 149–50). "The money must be newly minted and arranged according to denomination: ones, fives, tens, or twenties. The blankets are arranged in patterns based on symmetry: e.g. twelve bills across and fifteen down. Each blanket is edged by ribbon and flowers, real or silk" (150). When the procession stops in front of designated homes, St. Gerard's devotees emerge and slowly walk their decorated blankets to the street.

> The blankets of money they make to wrap around the saint's statue are so long that they have to roll them on large cardboard tubes used to wrap carpets. It often takes at least 45 minutes to an hour for Rafaello and Anna to complete wrapping the statue of the saint with the blankets they offer to him as a sign of their devotion. (Savastano 2011, 180)

As the processed statue is swathed with ever-increasing capes and blankets, it is said that "St. Gerard is gaining weight." The procession continues along its route through the city streets to return to the church where the money is collected and counted.

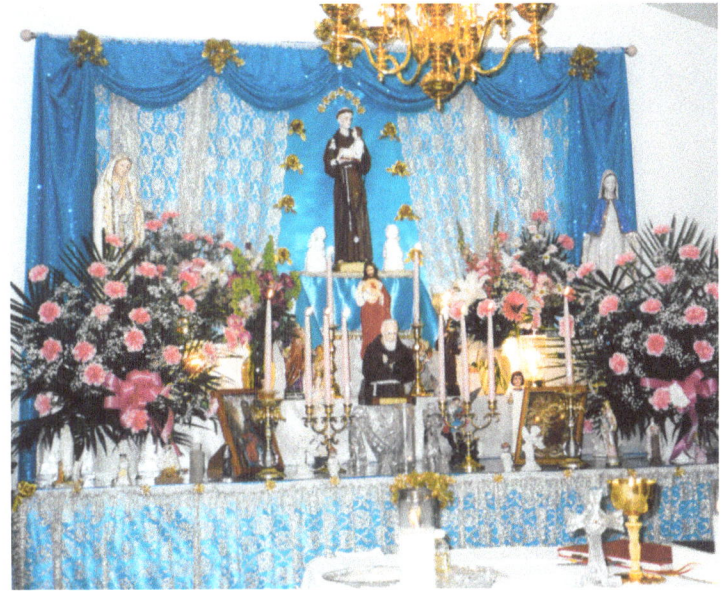

Angela Sanfillipo's home altar for St. Anthony assembled anew each year in her living room. Gloucester, Massachusetts, June 13, 2005.

Photo: Joseph Sciorra

Members of the Sicilian-American community in Gloucester, Massachusetts, create domestic votive altars or "tables" to St. Joseph and St. Anthony of Padua on the March 19th and June 13th feast days, respectively. Angela Sanfillipo, originally from Terrasini (Palermo province), turned to St. Anthony in 1975 when she and her fisherman husband, Giovanni, were struggling financially. "We had really hard times. We bought a boat that was junk, that brought us to the bottom. We prayed to St. Anthony to get us out of this mess" (telephone interview, June 10, 2005). Nina Groppo (Trappeto, Palermo province) began her annual altar to St. Joseph in 1995, after her mother was diagnosed with breast cancer.

> Believe it or not, instead of cancer, she had this fatty tumor, and the doctors up to today, still say, "You know, you received a miracle," because she had had I don't know how many cat-scans, how many pet-scans, how many ultrasounds, you name it. Ten doctors [said] it was cancer. And she went into the operating room, and thought they were going to remove her breast. They kept telling her that "depending on what we find we may have to." But thank the Lord, thank St. Joseph, thank all the saints, I mean really, she came out, no problem. And I had said to St. Joseph that I would do the altar. (interview, June 14, 2005)

Sanfillipo's and Groppo's respective altars assembled in 2005 shared many compositional elements that were learned through matrilineal tutelage: arranged vertically in three-tiered levels and horizontally with a bilateral, tripartite symmetry; use of drapery and patterned and/or lace cloth both for the curtained backdrop and the table skirt and surface covering; and inclusion of candles, vases of cut flowers, and statues and framed prints of celestial figures. At the pinnacle was a statue of the petitioned and feted saint. The altars were erected in living rooms where a priest celebrated mass, and the

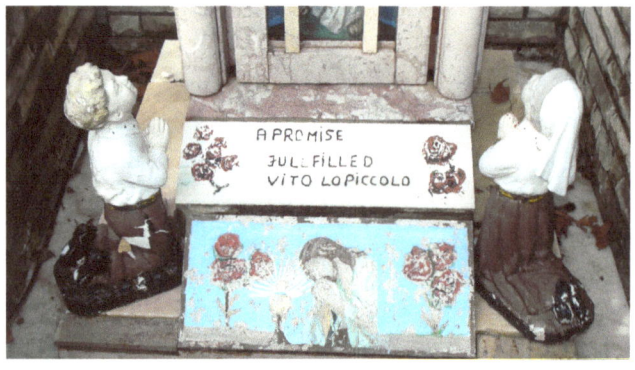

The base of Vito's LoPiccolo's yard shrine to St. Joseph, Dyker Heights, Brooklyn, October 2, 2011.

Photo: Joseph Sciorra

homes were open to the community at large for three days of communal prayer and hymns, as well as the culinary bounty of Sicilian delicacies offered as part of the social gathering.

The Italian-American sections of Brooklyn, New York, are noted for their well-built yard shrines, an adaptation of the structures known as *edicole sacre* found alongside country roads and on urban apartment buildings throughout Italy (see Sciorra 1989 and 1998). Often the more elaborate constructions are part of a specific votive act. In 1944, the Chinnici family of Gravesend commissioned a neighboring mason to build a fieldstone shrine to the Virgin in thanks for the safe return of sons serving in the military during World War II. In 1980, Rose Scarcella asked her husband Dominick to build a grotto in front of their Bensonhurst home after she prayed to the Blessed Mother on behalf of her son John, who overcame a seven-year battle with Hodgkin's disease. Standing in a lush flower garden, the Scarcella's grotto is bathed in a homemade waterfall and illuminated nocturnally with a soft blue spotlight. In 1985, Sicilian immigrant Vito LoPiccolo of Dyker Heights asked *paesano* Giovanni Galeoto to build a shrine of brick, marble, and wrought iron to St. Joseph, who was successfully petitioned to relieve a paralysis of the leg. When it was completed, LoPiccolo painted the words, "A Promise Fulfilled," and signed his name at the base of the shrine.

Ex-votos are the physical and public manifestation of the transcendental link between an individual and the divine. They are powerfully charged objects that resonate sympathetically with the anguish and affliction of maladies and near-death experiences. And they are infused with the sensual memory of those who once lovingly cradled and fervently clutched them before releasing the offerings in a sacred covenant. Even the lingering specters in photographs emanate a panoply of sensations—desperation, hope, yearning, joy, gratitude—of the ex-votos now long gone. These objects speak to us, they tell us stories, but only if we encourage them to do so. The question is whether we are receptive to listening and properly equipped to engage in dynamic conversation with these objects. Will their voices be strong, clear, and annunciated—or a faint, garbled mummer? For it is from these unpretentious yet evocative artifacts that a history of Italian-American Catholic sentiment and thought can be gleaned.

ACKNOWLEDGMENTS

I would like to thank Laura Caporrotti, Stephen La Rocca, Chiara Mazzuchelli, Rosaria Musco-Talone, Mark Pezzano, Stephanie Romeo, Serafina Rotondi, Laura Ruberto, Phyllis Tesoriero, and Ilaria Vanni for their assistance.

NOTES

1. This essay grows out of a long-standing interest in the material culture of Italian Americans, especially as it concerns religious belief and practice, e.g., Sciorra 1989, 1998, 2003, and 2004.

2. A perusal of Hobbie's directory of Italian-American material culture (1992) lists no known collection. See Carroll (1992, 82–87) for more information in English on *tavolette*.

3. A transcription of the original is as follows:

> And I prayed and I said, "If I get out of this wood, I gotta create a voto. *Fare un voto.* I gotta create a painting for myself." And so, *è quando mi rimisi, allora mi misi a pittare questo, che rappresenta il moribondo, diciamo così, quasi per morire. And che appare in cielo, la croce. La croce rappresenta tutte le cose che supportiamo sulla terra—tutti i guai, le pene, i dolori— è la croce. Che noi portiamo sempre per qualcosa che ci capita, è quella, la croce. Condonnati, che la dobbiamo portare per tutta la vita.*
>
> *Poi, la colomba della pace, che se dovevo morire c'è la pace. Con la columba vedi, porta, ah, entra dalla finestra e mentre lei entra le nuvole . . . se ne vanno, esce il sereno, cioè l'amalato si guarisce, sta meglio. È tutto perché è venuto il Signore e ha detto, "Alzate."* You understand? So in other words *è una composizione, non è un sogno, non è niente,* I mean *[non che non] è niente, è una stanza dove escono queste cose che in realtà non esistano ma nella fantasia, nella mia visione esistano.*
>
> [. . .]
>
> *Lo volevano comprare. Non è per vendere.* It's not for sale. *È mio. Lo tengo nella stanza da letto.*
>
> JS: It's beautiful.
>
> *Per me è che rappresenta molto. E tutto, diciamo cosi. Ognuno può giudicare come vuole, ma per me rappresenta una storia. È la mia storia.*

4. Perhaps Italian immigrant *tavolette* might be found in Latin America's predominately Catholic countries like Argentina, Brazil, and Venezuela.

5. A disproportionate number of the examples discussed here come from a single region, Piedmont, in northern Italy. This fact is attributed to my meager library collection and the nature of this preliminary research. Additional work needs to be conducted in Italian churches and museums to locate migration-themed *tavolette* from the Mezzogiorno, from where the vast majority of immigrants departed.

6. Maritime themes constitute an important ex-voto genre. See *Mariners' Votive Offerings in the Montenero Sanctuary* (1984) and Borg (2005).

7. See figures 3 and 38 for images of the Madonna of Oropa.

8. Additional information can be found in the back of Agosti's book under the listing "Elenco delle fotografie."

9. In an article on ex-votos at the Sanctuary of the Madonna of the Rosary, Eleonora Puntillo parenthetically mentions that "a photographic collage documents the on-the-job accident from which Vincenzo Pellone, 'New York, Brooklyn, April 1967,' emerged unscathed" (1995, 33).

10. The church and the street were destroyed in 1956 as part of the expansion of the Brooklyn Bridge

ramp. Three photographs (#U298608INP, May 15, 1925; #BE0333040, August 16, 1926; #BE027052, August 16, 1933) of a St. Roch feast in the Bettmann Archive (www.corbis.com; accessed April 13, 2011) are also from St. Joachim's Church. The descriptive title of Walker Evans's four photographs "Votive Candles, New York City" (1929–30) in the Metropolitan Museum of Art's collection (accession numbers: 1994.251.299, 1994.251.300, 1994.253.4.1, and 1994.253.4.2) states the images were taken on Roosevelt Street, perhaps during the feast to St. Roch (www.metmusuem.org; accessed April 14, 2011).

11. Giuseppe De Vita of Moio della Civitella (Salerno province), Campania, has posted online his dialect poem "La Centa" (partially quoted here), which briefly mentions the ex-voto constructed for a retuning emigrant:

La centa se facìa a la Maronna	*La centa* is made for the Madonna
re lo Monte ppe 'nno vuto.	of the Mountain as a vow.
Ppe 'nno figlio ca tornava	For the son who returned
sano ra la uèrra.	safe from the war.
Ppe 'nno marito ca tornava 'ncasa	For the husband who returned home
roppo trent'anni r'America.	after thirty years in America.
[. . .]	[. . .]
(De Vita 2007)	

12. Rubino inaccurately translates the dialect term *centa* to mean "hundred" from the Italian *cento*.

WORKS CITED

Agosti, Paola. 1979. *Immagine del mondo dei vinti*. Milan: Gabriele Mazzotta Editore.

Armstrong, Robert Plant. 1981. *The Powers of Presence: Consciousness, Myth, and Affecting Presence*. Philadelphia: University of Pennsylvania Press.

Bevilacqua, Piero, Andreina De Clementi, and Emilio Franzina, eds. 2002. "Memorie visive degli emigranti/Visual Memoirs of the Emigrants." Compact disc. In *Storia dell'emigrazione italiana: Arrivi*. Rome: Donzelli Editore.

Borg, Isabelle. 2005. *The Maritime Ex-Voto: A Culture of Thanksgiving in Malta*. Sta Venera, Malta: Heritage Books.

Carroll, Michael P. 1992. *Madonnas That Maim: Popular Catholicism in Italy Since the Fifteenth Century*. Baltimore: The Johns Hopkins University Press.

De Vita, Giuseppe. 2007. "La centa (Il cinto votivo)." Giuseppe De Vita da Moio della Civitella Salerno blog. June 8. http://wwwgiuseppedevita.blog.tiscali.it/2007/06/08/la_centa___il_cinto_votivo___1757998-shtml/?doing_wp_cron (accessed April 5, 2011).

Didi-Huberman, Georges. 2007. "Ex-Voto: Image, Organ, Time." *L'Esprit Créateur* 47(3): 7–16.

Dossena, Tiziano Thomas. 1995. "Natale Rotondi: L'essenza del colore." *L'Idea* Fall: 6–8.

Durant, Jorge, and Douglas Massy. 1995. *Miracles on the Border: Retablos of Mexican Migrants to the United States*. Tucson: The University of Arizona Press.

Freedberg, David. 1989. *The Power of Images: Studies in the History and Theory of Response*. Chicago: The University of Chicago Press.

Hobbie, Margaret. 1992. *Italian American Material Culture: A Directory of Collections, Sites, and Festivals in the United States and Canada*. New York: Greenwood Press.

IMAGES: A Pictorial History of Italian Americans. 1986. New York: The Center for Migration Studies of New York.

The Italians of New York. 1938. New York: Random House.

"'Little Italy' Cloaks Its Healing Saint in Dollars." 1937. *LIFE* September 6, 71–72.

Mariners' Votive Offerings in the Montenero Sanctuary/Ex voto marinari del Santuario di Montenero [exhibition catalog]. 1984. Philadelphia: Port of History Museum at Penn's Landing.

McDannell, Colleen. 1995. *Material Christianity: Religion and Popular Culture in America.* New Haven: Yale University Press.

Morgan, David. 1998. *Visual Piety: A History and Theory of Popular Religious Images.* Berkeley: University of California Press.

Orsi, Robert Anthony. 1985. *The Madonna of 115th Street: Faith and Community in Italian Harlem, 1880–1950.* New Haven: Yale University Press.

Puntillo, Eleonora. 1995. "Ex Votos." *Italy Italy* February–March, 26–33.

Rak, Michele, and Antonio Ermanno Giardino. 1987. *Il miracolo dipinto.* Naples: Sergio Civita Editore.

Rossi, Annabella. 1986. *Le feste dei poveri.* Palermo: Sellerio Editore.

Rubino, Mike. 1992. "Traditional Feast Ingredients." *Fra Noi* May, 37.

Rubino, Mike. 1987. "'La festa' Has a Language of Its Own." *Fra Noi* June 25, 3, 14.

"San Rocco Honored by Rival Factions" 1906. *New York Times,* August 17, 7.

Savastano, Peter. 2011. "Changing St. Gerard's Clothes: An Exercise in Italian-American Catholic Devotion and Material Culture." In *Italian Folk: Vernacular Culture in Italian-American Lives,* edited by Joseph Sciorra, 171–87. New York: Fordham University Press.

Savastano, Peter. 2002. "'Will the Real St. Gerard Please Stand Up?': An Ethnographic Study of Symbolic Polysemy, Devotional Practices, Material Culture, and Marginality and Difference in the Cult of St. Gerard Maiella." Dissertation. Drew University.

Sciorra, Joseph. 2004. "The Black Madonna of East Thirteenth Street." *Voices: The Journal of New York Folklore* 30(1–2): 14–17.

Sciorra, Joseph, ed. 2003. *Sacred Emblems, Community Signs: Historic Flags and Religious Banners from Italian Williamsburg, Brooklyn* [exhibition catalog]. New York: Casa Italiana Zerilli-Marimò, New York University.

Sciorra, Joseph. 1998. "Yard Shrines of Italian New York." (Photographs by Martha Cooper). *culturefront* Fall: 57–64.

Sciorra, Joseph. 1989. "Yard Shrines and Sidewalk Altars of New York's Italian-Americans." *Perspectives in Vernacular Architecture,* Volume III. Edited by Thomas Carter and Bernard L. Herman, 185–198. Columbia, Missouri: University of Missouri Press.

St. Rocco Society of Potenza. "Vows of Wax." http://stroccosociety.com/WaxParts.aspx (accessed June 2, 2011).

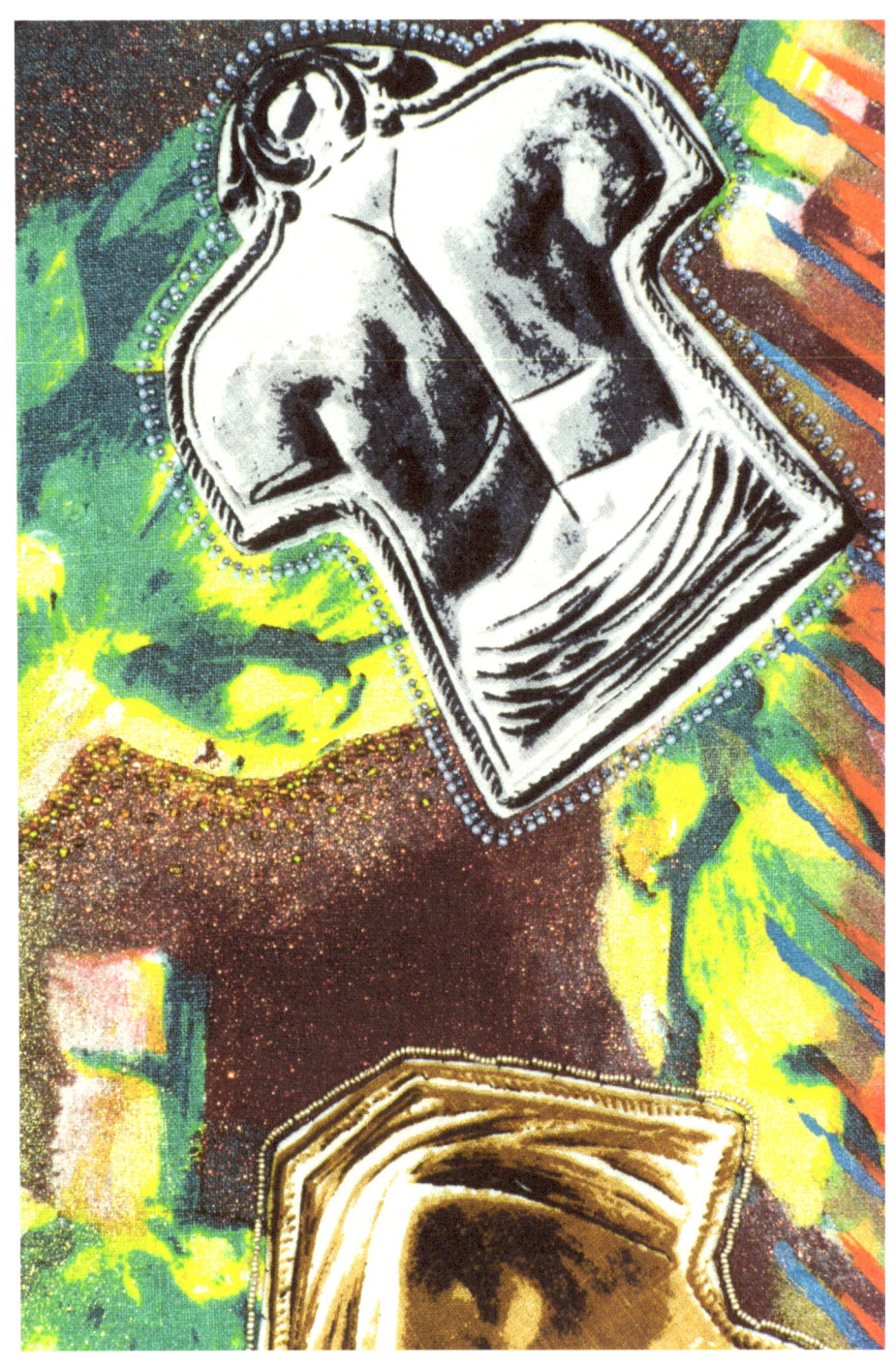

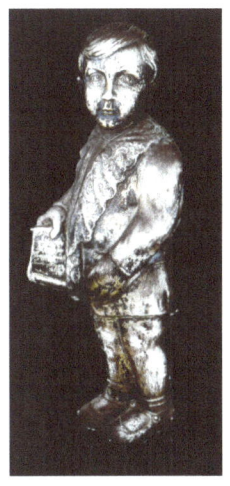

Laminae Ex-votos

RESONANT OBJECTS, SPIRITUAL MATERIALISM

KATE WAGLE

MATERIAL representation of body parts in the service of spiritual communication has its origins in ancient Mediterranean culture—a strong influence still in the sea-hemmed and history-infused regions of southern Italy. Such practices are directly connected to the function and imagery of contemporary "laminae" ex-votos, embossed metal sheets produced both mechanically and by individual craftspeople. The laminae ex-votos are "very modern" (Monsignor Pietro Caggiano, personal communication, September 6, 1996) in this continuum, with none readily identifiable earlier than the seventeenth century (Tripputi 1995, 10) and most dating from the nineteenth.

The physical and visual natures of the ex-voto in different towns reflect the peculiarities of local history and environment. For example, petitioners come from throughout the city and countryside to the sanctuary of Monte Pellegrino in Palermo, Sicily. The church is dedicated to St. Rosalia, the patron to whom the offerings are directed. "Ex-votos in silver are found everywhere: the most ancient already gathered in windows and glass showcases, laid around the simulation of the saint or hung in disorderly fashion on the most recent walls of the city" (Trupia 1984, 10).[1] Most are silver sheets (laminae) embossed with images including "eyes, nose, ears, arms, hands, fingers, legs (with and without feet), feet, abdomens, breasts, torsos, genitals, esophagus, lungs, kidneys, vertebral columns, uteruses etc." (Trupia 1984, 10).

While factory-stamped versions are numerous, handcrafted embossings still predominate to contemporary times. The craftspeople of Palermo are descended from a long and prestigious artisan tradition dating back to at least the eleventh century, where local patrons historically sought out silversmiths in the Tribunali–Castellamare neighborhood of the city. Dedicated to this purpose in the Middle Ages and called Argentaria, today the neighborhood continues to be an active destination of devotees seeking the "authenticity" and value of hand-worked ex-votos.

Opposite

Agnese (detail)
Marna Goldstein-Brauner
Printed textile, 2001

Above

Ex-voto, child
Francesco Pisapia
Silver, 23 inches (58 cm) height
Sanctuary of the Madonna of the
Rosary, Pompei
Photo: Araldo De Luca

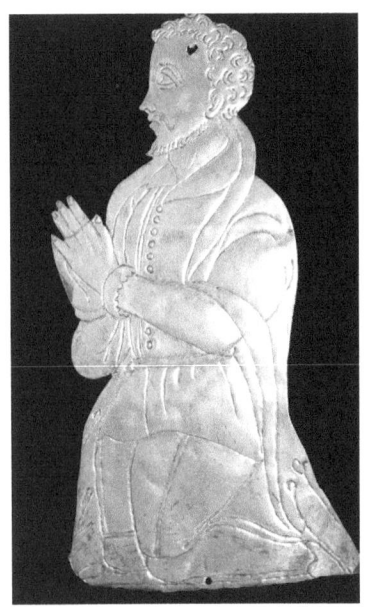

Ex-voto, man genuflecting
Silver
Gorga Collection, Museo
Nazionale delle Arti e Tradizione
Popolare, Rome
Photo: Kate Wagle

The economy of the region is another reason for the use of precious materials and processes. In an odd inversion of the predictable, poverty seems to dictate the richness of the expression here. While many devotees may be poor, "the greater the initial state of privation, the greater the entity of the gift will have to be—symbol of the opulence which springs up, for all to see, from the daily poverty" (Trupia 1984, 12).

Most of the ex-votos currently displayed at the Sanctuary of the Madonna of the Arch in Sant'Anastasia, outside of Naples, appear to date from the ninetieth and twentieth centuries and include masses of handmade and mass-produced sheet-silver reliefs of every scale and description. A large area of the sanctuary contains ex-votos depicting war scenes, while other areas are organized and patterned via systems that range from clusters of like objects (children, hands, arms, horses, etc.) to chronology (the most contemporary examples are grouped together). Enormous wooden panels cut to fit the arcs of entries at each end of the collection space contour dense arrangements of laminae ex-votos—figures, legs, hands, hearts, etc.—both identical and varied, mounted by workmen at the direction of the priests.

In contrast, the nearby Sanctuary of the Madonna of the Rosary in Pompei was deliberately founded in the late nineteenth century as a dignified manifestation of the wealth and rationality of the industrial age, "where the rich and noble families of Naples could worship together with the local farmers" (Puntillo 1995, 33). Constructed between 1876 and 1887, the sanctuary was conceived as a missionary work, directed at a poverty-burdened peasant culture that was still "in contact with the remains of paganism springing from the fields of the ancient Pompeii" (Rak 1990, 86) and so tested the limits of the church's ideological tolerance. Initially the sanctuary's clergy openly disapproved of the offerings of braids, wax feet, and eyes favored by the devotees. However, the merger of belief systems produced a tradition that, while it belongs wholly to the "industrial age, connected in its moments of foundation, diffusion, and stabilization with the logic of industrialism's system of information" (Rak 1990, 53), is simultaneously a Marian cult, anchored by icons of the Madonna of the Rosary that correlate to ancient paganism, evident from images of a child, a crescent moon, and a heart, among others.

An illustration of the dual identity is offered in a business-like accounting of the carefully documented record of graces (miracles attributed to the portrait of the Madonna of the Rosary transported by cart from Naples in 1875):

If we look at the figures on a three yearly basis, we can see that an average of 4 graces per year are documented between 1876 and 1878, which soon become 38 between 1879 and 1881, 438 between 1882 and 1884, and an astonishing 1,119 per year between 1885 and 1887, with consequent, striking increases in the percentages for each 3 year period: 950% (1879–1881), 1,152% (1882–1884) and then dropping to a more moderate rate, stabilizing after the initial boom. (Turchini 1990, 111)

The figures are attributed not only to the miraculous powers of the icon but also to the effectiveness and wide distribution of *Il Rosario e la Nuova Pompei*, a newspaper published by Bartolo Longo, the founder of the sanctuary. As the numbers mounted, publicity surrounding a whole range of miracles drew more ex-votos. The newly formed church adapted to its environment and now houses a remarkable collection of material expressions of gratitude.

In an odd inversion of the predictable, poverty seems to dictate the richness of the expression here

Ex-votos are visible in several areas of the sanctuary in Pompei. The oldest date to the year the church was opened (Monsignor Pietro Caggiano, personal communication, September 6, 1996). More than 3,000 laminae are mounted high on the walls in eight lunettes around the transept, placed there by nuns when the sanctuary was restructured in 1939—repeated versions of silver hearts, figures, and body parts fill these thickly textured fields and punctuate the architectural interior. A gallery of immaculate glass cases houses other categories of mostly three-dimensional objects, including a number of life-sized, cast-silver infants. An extraordinary collection of highly personalized offerings occupies the halls of the church office area, frames and cases illuminated by the greenish glow of fluorescent tubes. These presentations of silver sheets, paintings, photographs, embroidery, fabric, human hair, and objects, often organized as collage, are dramatically illustrated insights into the history of this community and of the laminae ex-votos. All are evidence that the new record "is different from the ancient one and powerfully exposed to industrialism's new means of communication—photography, magazines, the first forms of publicity and above all an astonishing hyper-production of objects." This tradition now makes use of materials, processes, and icons "from the new catalog offered by this great artificial nature constructed by industrial society" (Rak 1990, 54).

The Industrial Revolution defines the physical and visual nature of all of these collections. While mass production of "stylized human figures, body parts, inner organs, animals, plants and personal items" (Egan 1991, 11) was common by the Middle Ages in Western Europe, the metal objects of that era were primarily cast or worked by hand:

> Man-made artifacts could always be imitated by men. Replicas were made by pupils in practice of their craft, by masters for diffusing their works, and, finally, by third parties in pursuit of gain. Mechanical reproduction of a work of art, however represents something new. Historically, it advanced intermittently and in leaps at long intervals, but with accelerated intensity. (Benjamin 1968, 220)

The thin sheets of silver used in the production of votive objects are themselves the laminae, produced by industrial rolling mills in modern facilities. In the eighteenth and nineteenth centuries Italian silver was "still more decorative and extravagantly ornamental" (Stobart 1995, 57) than that produced by northern European craftsmen, including religious objects that were being produced in quantity in southern Italian workshops. Those decorative influences, particularly of the various stylistic revivals that proliferated in this era, are still evident in the elaborate and beautifully stylized images of contemporary laminae ex-votos, of which the sanctuary at Pompei may have as many as 10,000 repetitions of some forms. Flat-silver ex-votos started to be industrially produced "around 1880" (Father Giuseppe Petagna, personal communication, September 6, 1996). Though many continued to be handmade by traditional repoussé techniques, the low relief of the sheet form is particularly adaptable to production stamping processes. Industrial production of laminae ex-votos seems primarily centered in northern Italy, yet individual craftspeople still produce commissioned works in the south.

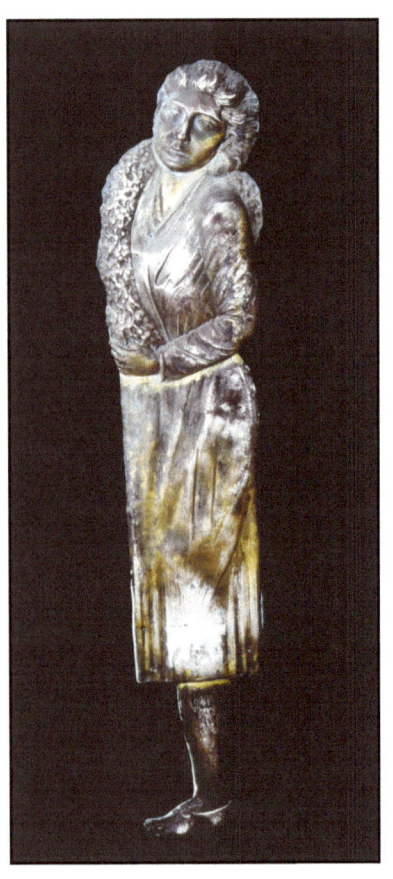

Ex-voto, woman
Francesco Pisapia
Silver, 59 inches (150 cm) height
Sanctuary of the Madonna of the
Rosary, Pompei
Photo: Araldo De Luca

In Palermo silversmiths, embossers, goldsmiths, and engravers are responsible for seven phases of a sequence described as "fusion" (alloying 1,000 grams of pure silver to 250 grams copper, lowered greatly from the sterling-level standard set by Frederick II in the thirteenth century), "lamination," "shaping," "embossment," "refinishing," "silvering," and "polishing" referred to as *il miracolo* ("the miracle") (Trupia 1984, 27–33). As part of this process the artisan and the devotee participate in an intense collaboration of craft and content. The craftsperson's skills are engaged on several levels; technically, in terms of process, regarding knowledge of the codified catalog of reference provided by traditional forms, and, as a confidante, in that the silversmith offers "his interested attention to the story" (Trupia 1984, 13) of his client. In this remarkable interaction "the devoted speaks of himself without reserve" (13), and the artisan and client are united in "solidarity and complicity" (13) in opposition to the church's "persecutorial attitude" (13) toward the ex-voto tradition. The process is prolonged, with multiple visits to view progress and make changes. In this way, the two parties cooperate. The silversmith's expertise is applied to the development of an object that manifests the devotee's deep spiritual response to a miraculous event.

The personal nature of this process influences the gradual evolution and alteration of the metal forms, since details of the narrative that alter the traditional can be readily integrated by the silversmith with a fluidity unavailable in industrial production. However, the pressure of industrial forces is another important factor. Both mechanically produced and hand-formed silver ex-votos exhibit similar changes in recent years. It isn't possible to identify authorship of innovations since the factory

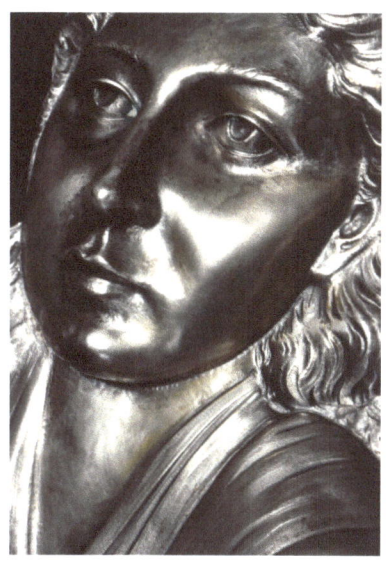

Detail of ex-voto, opposite

can quickly adopt an artisan's modification and reproduce it on a large scale. In turn, the silversmith is as likely to appropriate a manufactured device (from the manufactured models kept in stock for clients who prefer them) and incorporate it into future practice. However, some major trends can be identified over the years. Earlier examples include more handcrafted, detailed, large-scale sheet objects fabricated of silver and occasionally gold. A full-scale woman and small child of hammered silver are stunning examples from the sanctuary in Pompei. The personal immediacy of the figures (see page 55 top and opposite) implies portraiture rather than stylization, and the marks of hammers and tools are used with great facility to render subtle details and modeling in the sheet relief.

Later examples tend to be mechanically produced, hand-scale forms of silver-plated alloys. It is difficult to generalize regarding the quality of industrially stamped laminae over time. Even two mechanically produced samples of the same image, both available for contemporary purchase, offer comparisons of imagery and workmanship. In these pieces both the materials, one piece sterling and the other plated, and the die makers' skill in rendering details of hair and subtleties of modeling demonstrate an obvious range of outcomes via industrial processes. More recently laminae are incorporated into collage formats, due in part to the availability of a new material culture. "With industrialism the symbolic object began to count above all, as the precious materials slowly became property of the masses, and therefore no longer objects of particular worth" (Rak 1990, 79).

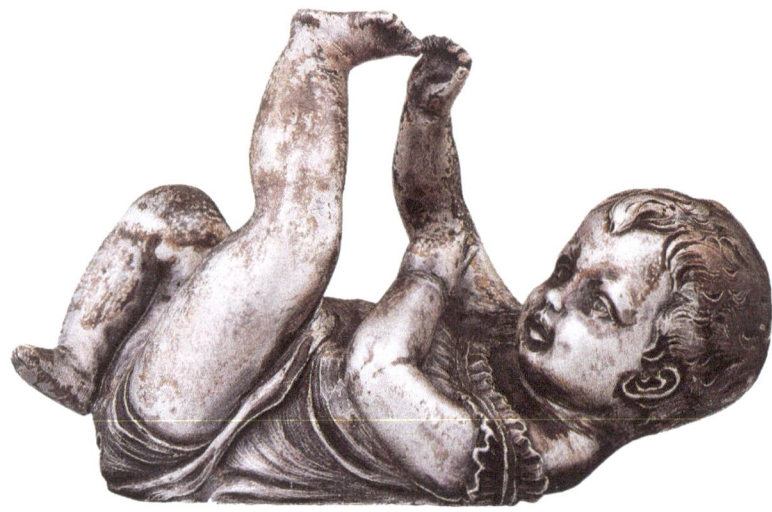

Ex-voto, baby
Silver, 59 inches (150 cm) width
Sanctuary of the Madonna of the
Rosary, Pompei
Photo: Araldo De Luca

While the laminae may be symbolic, they are within the culture "sensible things, objects" (Monsignor Pietro Caggiano, personal communication, September 6, 1996)—not aesthetic, but functional forms. Parts of the actual body are equally precious, i.e., hair or gallstones. Historically, the source of much laminae ex-voto imagery is the belief that fragments of the devotee's body are the most personal gift, testament to an impossible obstacle miraculously overcome. At the turn of the twentieth century the "new Madonna" at Pompei was offered "the equivalent weight in silver of the child who had recovered by means of blessing, and devotees nailed thin silver sheets to the wall reproducing the parts of the body struck by illness" (Rak 1990, 53). The sculptural baby (above) was produced by skilled workers and speaks to an ancient custom of the devout traditions. The weight of the child was in this instance precious metal, but the practice did not exclude other materials; "some groups offered their weight in cheese and meat, bread and vegetables" (Rak 1990, 76).

The metal sheets are signs of the disease, the sick part of the body "auspiciously detached from the body of the devotee and displayed in the sacred place where they could no longer harm, crystallized in the incorruptible material" (Rak 1990, 86). Many elements of this symbolic body have survived intact from ancient cultures and reference very diverse devotional practices. The body is rendered in three different modes: "the body of small parts and of internal organs—eyes, lips, breasts, kidneys, lungs, intestines, hands and feet; the body of large parts—the head, chest, back, abdomen, legs and arms; and the body of the entire figure" (86). Almost all these parts refer to a popular ancient anatomy and are synecdoche—parts put for the whole—of illnesses that have struck a zone. The more specialized anatomic details, as the kidneys, the lungs, or the intestines, are of more recent design. The heart, however, doesn't necessarily indicate an organ, but is an emblem of sacrifice, recurring in the Christian tradition throughout

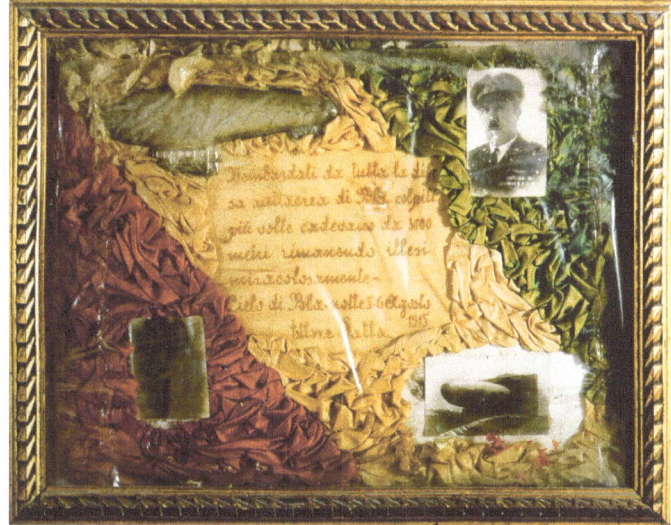

Ex-voto
Satin tri-color flag with three
photographs, airship in silver
lamina, and embroidered writing
19½ x 26 inches (48.5 x 65.5 cm)
Sanctuary of the Madonna of the
Rosary, Pompei
Photo: Araldo De Luca

its history. As ex-voto, it seldom appears alone, but in pictures, tied to cut braids, baby ribbons, photographs, and other contextual materials. Other common images include houses, horses, food, and animals. Some vehicles are also part of the collections of laminae.

Whole figures are used often. There are two recurring types of female figure whose dress and attitude point to origins in differing time periods. One masculine figure is a drapery-clad child linked visually to antiquity. A female child wears a short dress. Other male figures wear suits and military uniforms. Newly manufactured soldiers still wear old uniforms—the vocabulary of war seems not to require a specific time frame. In fact, there are few if any laminae that manifest contemporary images, although other new metal forms are evolving. At the Sanctuary of the Madonna of the Arch, a number of ex-votos incorporate beautifully fabricated gold hypodermic needles, visual testimony to recent deliverance from drug addiction.

The old forms are increasingly combined with new materials of mass culture. Over the last century photography became an important element of a new model. Devotees developed a language of ex-votos in collage that articulated a specific narrative. For example, an ex-voto that has as its subject an airship accident (above) is displayed at the sanctuary of the Madonna of the Rosary. The aircraft is rendered both in silver and as a photograph. A second photograph is of the devotee and an inscription describes the event: *"Bombarded by the whole Ala² anti-aircraft defense, they were hit several times, then fell from a height of 3000m and were miraculously unhurt. Sky of Pola, on the night of 5–6th August 1915. Ettore Satta"* (Caggiano, Rak, and Turchini 1990, 160). All are masterfully organized in a tri-colored field of rippled satin.

Offerings often included newspaper clippings mixed with objects of the new material language, which utilize printed materials, medals, certificates, degrees, and hand-written narratives. The most frequent sequence includes the photo of the devotee, a small image, a silver plate, and a typescript. "This montage of images, writing, decoration and objects has, as a model, the material language of publicity and of its displays, the show windows" (Rak 1990, 77). In this way the ex-votos have become frank reflections of contemporary culture. They chronicle experience with a vocabulary that parallels the structures of both visual art and literature.

Affinities: Contemporary Art and the Ex-voto Vocabulary

Many aspects of this practice invite comparisons with secular modes of expression. The use of photography, painting, and collage as a format for presentation of the laminae objects directly corresponds to formats of extant visual art. The collections of mechanically reproduced objects mounted as masses of texture and testimony relate strongly to the concerns of contemporary art installation, offering some of the same opportunities for the creation of a conceptually charged environment through the visual organization of materials.

Over the last thirty years in the United States, craftspeople have shifted their attention to art and embraced the eclectic philosophies of postmodernism. Many contemporary artists in these fields show conceptual, sculptural, and environmental works, paralleling developments of nonobjective work in all visual disciplines. Protocols of other media and the media themselves are freely accessed by makers who have matured in an era that values interdisciplinary awareness. Resulting works quote sculpture and painting and incorporate photography, paper, fibers, paint, and other materials. They re-think traditional formats of adornment and vessel, shift scale from the familiarly miniature to the unavoidably gigantic, and quote and contextualize objects produced by cultures from around the world. The values of craft itself are systematically challenged by artists who understand that the "quality" of crafting is relative to the nature of the inquiry. All of the forms and traditions of the medium are open to question with a resulting exponential expansion of the field, blurring of traditional boundaries between disciplines, and intense scrutiny of cultural influences and meaning.

For example, ceramic artist Nancy Blum and Marna Goldstein-Brauner, whose medium is printed textiles, have in common a strong sense of materiality and an interest in the cultural and philosophical messages carried by materials and their worked forms. Each is also interested in image, in synthesizing pictorial renderings that relate to the natural world. The ex-voto tradition is intensely pictorial, relying on the power of recognizable images to carry a convincing message. In addition, both utilize the body in various aspects of their work.

The values of craft itself are systematically challenged by artists who understand that the "quality" of crafting is relative to the nature of the inquiry.

The body is our principal reference for understanding the physical world, both through our senses and as a referent for scale. The world from an Anglo-American perspective is measured by the body, in terms of hands and feet, distances from noses to fingertips. Ceramic practice embraces the subject of the figure from its earliest history. In relation to votive objects, clay tablets featuring ceramic renderings of figures and body parts also have their origins in ancient Mediterranean cultures. Nancy Blum fixes the clay objects she builds to the walls of an art gallery, rather than those of a temple. She refers to both the body and the votive tradition in many of her pieces. While the forms are familiar, Blum exaggerates their scale, moving our encounter into a mythical realm of understanding. Susan Stewart addresses this quality of "the gigantic" which can be viewed as "fantastic—an enlargement in the exterior of an interior emotion" (Stewart 1993, 82). The hands in *Hands Hansa* recall a traditional votive form in many details but are twice the length of a normal hand. They contradict the scale of Italian laminae ex-votos that tend to miniaturize or to assume a relatively human scale. Regarding the miniature and its capacity to present an experience of interior reflection, Stewart says "that the world of things can open itself to reveal a secret life—is a constant daydream that the miniature represents" (Stewart 1993, 54). The scale of ex-votos engage this intimate dream world. In contrast *Hands Hansa* constitutes a kind of spectacle, communicating a greatness of being, outside of common experience.

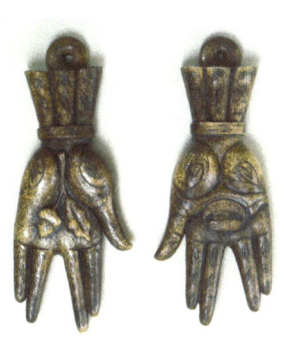

Hands Hansa
Nancy Blum
Ceramic, 1996

According to Blum's artist statement, "craft-informed sculpture is how I think of what I make. By carving surfaces that demand tactile engagement and constructing situations in which pieces can be moved or re-ordered, I have intentionally tried to involve the viewer in the aspect of art making I find most compelling, physical engagement" (Blum, personal communication, 1998). It is possible, then, to think of Blum's objects as functional sculpture. She encourages viewers to handle the smaller pieces. She believes that physical accessibility is critical for the communication of her intent. "By experiencing through our hands as well as our eyes, the pattern, texture and weight of these objects, we come to know the artist's hands. In our hands we re-experience

Blum's obsessive labors" (Nasisse 1998, 32), which directly echo the intensive personal and physical process of the handmade silver votive.

The skin of these pieces is the site of an additional layer of symbolic reference idiosyncratic to Blum and her work. The surface is intricately carved, embodying Blum's "emphasis on art as hard work" (Blum, personal communication, 1998). This mindfulness to complexity also offsets that aspect of gigantism that distances the individual and recalls the grotesque. "The more complicated the object, the more intricate, and the more these complexities and intricacies are attended to, the 'larger' the object is in significance" (Stewart 1993, 89). The detailed, labor-intensive surface also introduces another concern and a deeper connection to the use of votives as a focusing device for repetitive prayer and meditation. Andy Nasisse, in his article "The Sculpture of Nancy Blum," comments on this aspect of her work:

> The assumption is that movement and change in the physical world are synchronized with their counterpart in the metaphysical world. Our participation in the physical process of repetitive movement can become like a meditation. And in most meditations the constant repetition of a chant or a physical movement is the channel through which the mind expands. (Nasisse 1998, 31)

Marna Goldstein-Brauner is intrigued by the decorative quality of cloth, its utilitarian value and history of meaning and faith. She finds it difficult to think of fabric outside of a practical context, even if its purpose is not immediately evident. Still, she endeavors, as she writes in her artist statement, "to make cloth that is magical, that transcends the processes used to make it, while honoring a lengthy worldwide history of magic cloth making" (Goldstein-Brauner, personal communication, 2001). Her work is concerned with a history of textiles and human culture, particularly focusing on cloth as a ritual object. She considers herself a storyteller, conveying narrative experiences by developing relationships of decorative, pictorial imagery on textiles.

The ex-voto is also primarily "a communication" (Monsignor Pietro Caggiano, personal communication, September 6, 1996), "a collection of symbol models, which may be utilized as vehicles and channels with which to communicate with the sacred. The language of the ex-voto" (Rak 1990, 95). One aspect of this communicative nature is addressed by Pietro Caggiano in a publication from the Madonna of the Rosary. He warns:

> During the era of "social communication" one must avoid the potential dangers of the "depletion of the sign." The miracle is . . . an objective sign, that is rooted in the "fact," not merely tied to the judgment of those who have the power to accept or reject it. (Caggiano 1990, 23)

This statement, referring to the authenticity of the sign, gains aesthetic currency when related to literary structures outlined by Roland Barthes in his essay "Myth Today"

(Barthes 1972, 113). He assumes a commonality of experience that lends conviction to intentionally contextualized communications. Speaking of signifier and sign he describes the *signifier*, a bunch of roses, as "empty" without the *signified* . . . in his example, passion. It (the bunch of roses) becomes a "full" *sign,* through the author's intention and the references and associations provided by society's conventions and traditions. The evolving ex-voto tradition of the last twenty years provides innumerable illustrations of a similar use of object language. For example, the simple juxtaposition of an x-ray of real lungs anchored by a silver "mother" figure indicates a complex and poignant narrative without the use of written language.

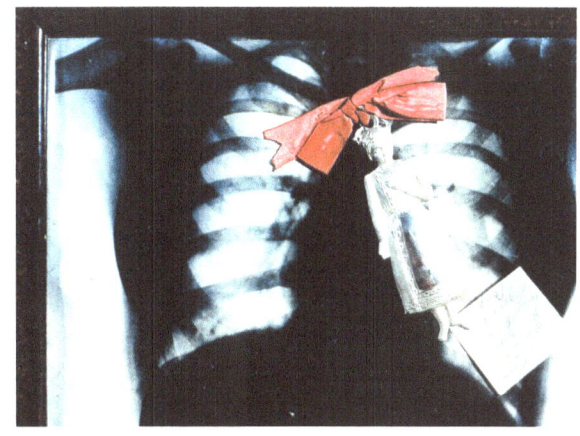

Ex-voto (detail)
Silver lamina with x-ray
Sanctuary of the Madonna of the Rosary, Pompei
Photo: Kate Wagle

In contrast, Goldstein-Brauner intends to raise questions regarding where her textiles exist in time and how they might function. As an artist she specifically invites the judgment of "those who have the power to accept or reject" (Goldstein-Brauner, personal communication, 2001). She plays contemporary photographic process and image against recognizably historical surfaces and formats, soliciting individual interpretation in the context of current art discourse.

The use of photography, painting, and collage in more contemporary ex-votos is a language in common with Goldstein-Brauner's work, in which the use of photography and xerography (copy-machine reproduction) allows her to capture "images that are real objects in a real world" (Goldstein-Brauner, personal communication 2001) and "install" these objects, including laminae ex-votos, onto planes of cloth that are richly patterned and decorated, yet manipulated by the artist to an appearance of age and wear.

Contemporary theory strengthens this connection between art and culture. In *On Photography* Susan Sontag argues that "to photograph is to appropriate the thing photographed. It means putting oneself into a certain relation to the world that feels like knowledge and, therefore like power" (Sontag 1977, 4).

Goldstein-Brauner's work intersects with these assertions in several areas. She chooses objects such as statuary and even the images of Italian laminae ex-votos, accessing their "realness" by transferring their accurate photographic representations to her elaborately conceived textile environments. By choosing these objects she appropriates a "glow—the quality of unknown ritual intent" (Goldstein-Brauner, personal communication, 2001) and refers to a sense of mystical power that attracted her to Jewish and Coptic textiles.

There are other corresponding ideas that inform both religious ritual and art practice. Walter Benjamin, in his essay "Art in the Age of Mechanical Reproduction" says that "artistic production begins with ceremonial objects destined to serve in a cult." Futhermore:

> Originally the contextual integration of art in tradition found its expression in the cult. We know that the earliest art works originated in the service of ritual—first the magical, then the religious kind. It is significant that the existence of the work of art with reference to its aura is never entirely separated from its ritual function. In other words, the unique value of the "authentic" work of art has its basis in ritual. (Benjamin 1968, 223)

The ex-voto ritual objects span the entire arc of the history, from magical to industrial production, that Benjamin cites and can be examined in relation to this concept of the "authentic." As ancient models of devotion declined, new models have been synthesized with aura intact and authenticity redescribed. The sanctuary at Pompei was particularly affected by the phenomenon of increased contact with the new systems of information and their constructions of image. It was programmed from the beginning to be open to contemporary changes and lacked elaborate codes of prohibitions, and so was very receptive to new varieties of devout expression. Benjamin contends that "that which withers in the age of mechanical reproduction is the aura of the work of art," and that reproductions substitute "a plurality of copies for a unique existence" (Benjamin 1968, 221).

However, the evidence of contemporary devotional objects and their visible influence in new aesthetic genres point instead to an embrace of mechanical reproduction for ritual purposes. The authenticity and "aura" of the ex-voto is preserved through "the growth of the devotee's personal labor" and newly interpretive discrimination in their presentation and composition. The contemporary ex-voto provides "proof of the search for an individual and unrepeatable contact" (Benjamin 1968, 223), often characterized by the use and re-purposing of mass-produced materials.

While the use of sign and symbol in the ex-voto tradition is intended to provide instant, transparent legibility, its close links to the prevailing culture lead inevitably to tension between ritual formulas and "the pulling deviation of ever new devotees who transfer to the inside of the sanctuary forms and models from the periphery of civil life" (Rak 1990, 96). Over time the conflict between church and community mounts until traditional forms are visibly altered, rendering those that came before illegible: "Hence, the repeated restructuring of many sanctuary interiors and the concealment of entire sections of ex-voto, such as wedding gowns, orthopedic apparatus, coffins, cut hair" (Rak 1990, 96) and the use of a new "combination of the irregular and the incoher-

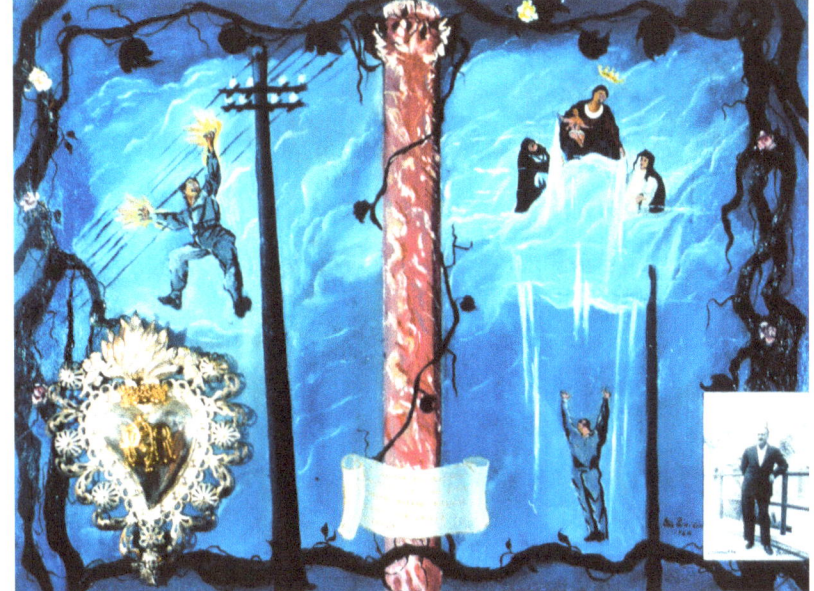

Ex-voto depicting powerline accident
Painting with silver lamina and photograph
Sanctuary of the Madonna of the Rosary, Pompei
Photo: Kate Wagle

ent in the objects of Artificial Nature" (80). The ambiguous messages that result from breaking the rules of a code and characterize this "combining" process suggest another shared structure with poetry and visual art. Terence Hawkes, elaborating on Umberto Eco's *A Theory of Semiotics* (1976), describes art as:

> A way of connecting "messages" together, in order to produce "texts" in which the "rule breaking" roles of ambiguity and self-reference are fostered and organized so that, as Umberto Eco sees it,
>
>> a. many messages on different levels are ambiguously organized
>>
>> b. the ambiguities follow a precise design
>>
>> c. both the normal and ambiguous devices in any one message exert a contextual pressure on the normal and ambiguous devices in all the others
>>
>> d. the way in which the "rules" of one system are violated by one message is the same as that in which the rules of another system are violated by their messages. (Eco 1976, 271)
>
> The effect is to generate an "aesthetic idiolect," or more plainly a "special language" peculiar to the work of art, which induces in its audience a sense of "cosmicity" . . . that is, of endlessly moving beyond each established level of meaning the moment it is established—of continuously transforming "its denotations into new connotations." (Hawkes 1977, 116)

Art (perhaps good art) does exactly this, and comprehension oscillates in spaces between image, content, and material. Some ex-voto compositions, though generated from a traditional image vocabulary, and often framed in specific narrative, have this character as well.

Even still shots from family photo albums, the kind that find their way into the ex-voto, have been characterized as profoundly ideological statements in that they bear witness to the typical in our culture. In *Snapshot Versions of Life*, Richard Chalfen speaks of "Kodak culture" and notes the snapshots connections to "folk art," as well as the authenticity of experience that they represent (Chalfen 1987, 71). In *On Photography*, Susan Sontag makes a number of assertions regarding snapshots—among these that they are "memento mori," "collectible objects . . . souvenirs of daily life," and "a social rite, a defense against anxiety, and a tool of power" (Sontag 1977, 6, 8, 15).

This description matches exactly the conceptual and visual idiosyncrasies of recent ex-voto forms and the contemporary art works that reference them. This new relational aesthetic is in marked contrast to the specificity of earlier models and has moved beyond the local. In this context, the individual messages of the laminae ex-voto are sublimated to a personal sense of overall narrative and visual composition and employ an eloquent vernacular of image, text, and disembodied object. Use of the silver sheets alone has declined over the last fifty years, and they have become esoteric "collectibles." However, within new organizations they retain their meaning as specific signs, serve as references to multiple histories—industry, tradition, and ritual, constitute a resource for contemporary artists, and retain an ineffable numinous "aura," the authority of their potent cultural history.

NOTE

1. All translations are my own.

2. The embroidered word appears to be "Pola," a town in Campania, not "Ala" as it appears in the quoted book.—Ed.

WORKS CITED

Barthes, Roland. 1972. *Mythologies*. New York: Hill and Wang.

Benjamin, Walter. 1968. "The Work of Art in the Age of Mechanical Reproduction." In *Illuminations*, edited by Hannah Arendt, 219–53. New York: Harcourt, Brace & World.

Caggiano, Pietro. 1990. "Theology of the Ex Voto." In *Sweet Mother*, edited by Peter Caggiano, Michele Rak, and Angelo Turchini, 15–30. Pompei: Pontifical Sanctuary of Pompeii.

Caggiano, Pietro, Michele Rak, and Angelo Turchini. 1990. *Sweet Mother*. Pompei: Pontifical Sanctuary of Pompeii.

Chalfen, Richard. 1987. *Snapshot Versions of Life*. Bowling Green, OH: Bowling Green State University Popular Press.

Eco, Umberto. 1976. *A Theory of Semiotics*. Bloomington, IN: Indiana University Press.

Egan, Martha. 1991. *Milagros: Votive Offerings from the Americas*. Santa Fe: Museum of New Mexico Press.

Hawkes, Terence. 1977. *Structuralism and Semiotics*. Berkeley: University of California Press.

Nasisse, Andy. 1998. "The Sculpture of Nancy Blum." *Ceramics: Art and Perception*, No. 33: 30–32.

Puntillo, Eleanora. 1995. "Ex Votos, of Grace and Gratitude." *Italy Italy* 13(1): February/March: 26–33.

Rak, Michele. 1990. "The Language of the Ex Voto." In *Sweet Mother*, edited by Peter Caggiano, Michele Rak, and Angelo Turchini, 51–100. Pompei: Pontifical Sanctuary of Pompeii.

Sontag, Susan. 1977. *On Photography*. New York: Farrar, Straus and Giroux.

Stewart, Susan. 1993. *On Longing: Narratives of the Miniature, the Gigantic, the Souvenir, the Collection*. Durham, NC: Duke University Press.

Stobart, Janet. 1995. "Silver for all Seasons." *Italy Italy* 13(1): February/March: 51–57.

Tripputi, Anna Maria. 1995. *Bibliografia degli* ex-voto. Bari: Paolo Malagrino Editore.

Trupia, Joli Scavone. 1984. *Itinerario di un Cuore,* Ex-voto *e argentieri a Palermo*. Palermo: Folkstudio di Palermo.

Turchini, Angelo. 1990. "Ordinary Stories and Sacred History." In *Sweet Mother*, edited by Peter Caggiano, Michele Rak, and Angelo Turchini, 101–130. Pompei: Pontifical Sanctuary of Pompeii.

Catalog

FIGURE 1

SILVERPLATE WITH BEADS
4¼ x 3 INCHES (10.5 x 7.5 CM)

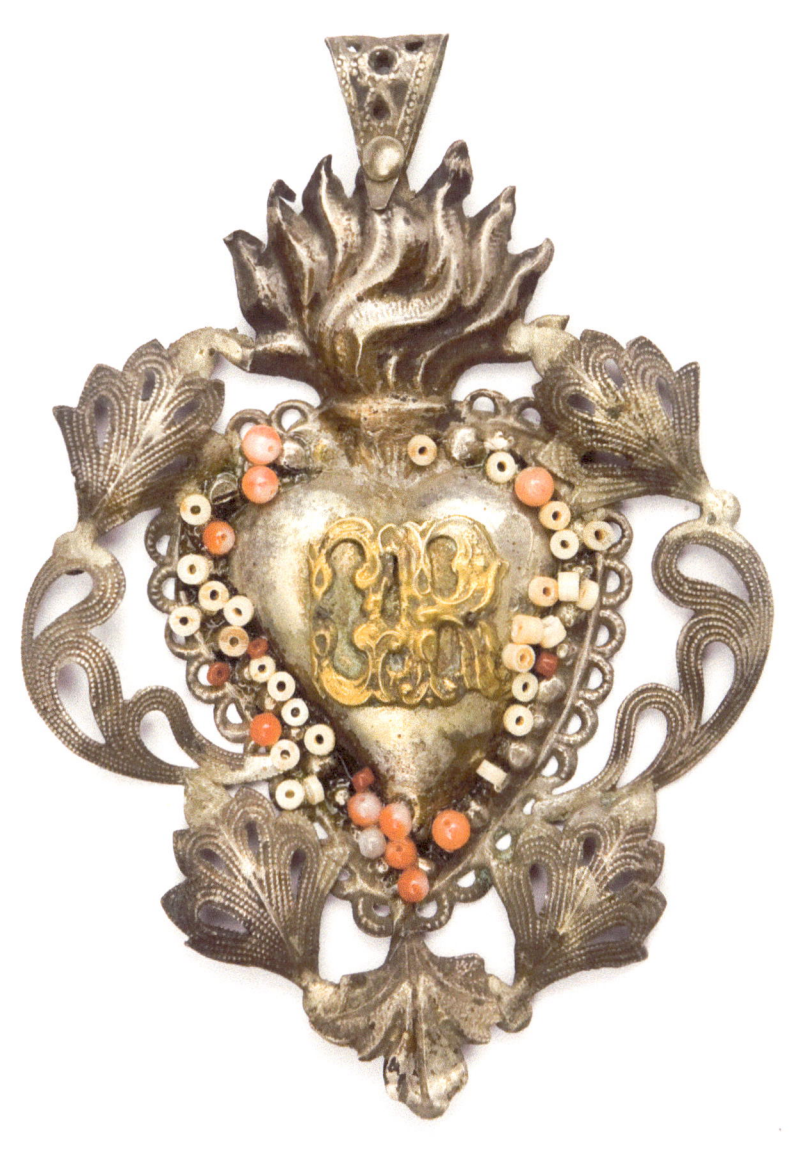

FIGURE 2

OIL ON WOOD

14¼ x 10¾ INCHES (36 x 27.5 CM)

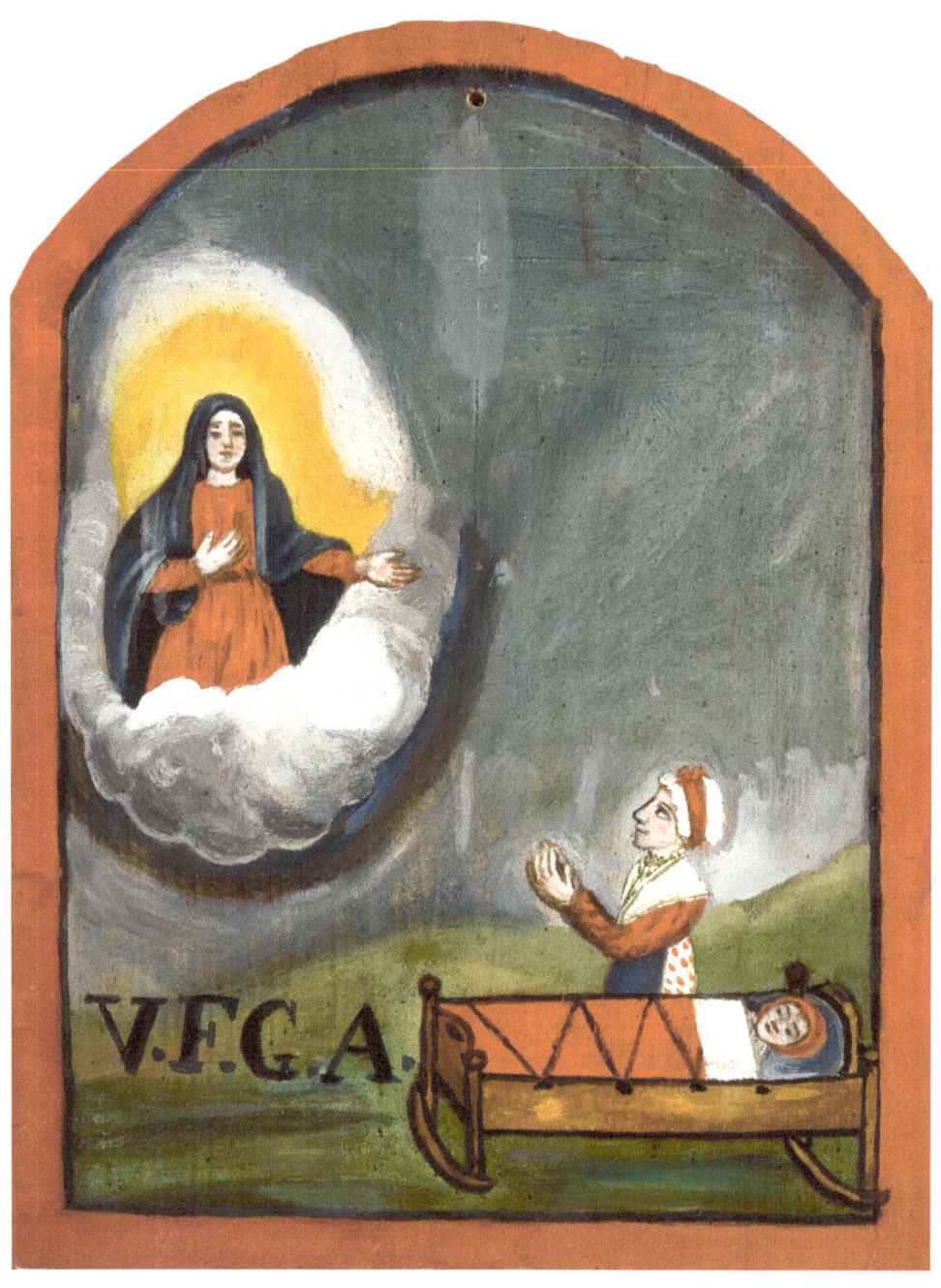

V.F.G.A.

FIGURE 3

OIL ON METAL

12 X 9 INCHES (30.5 X 23 CM)

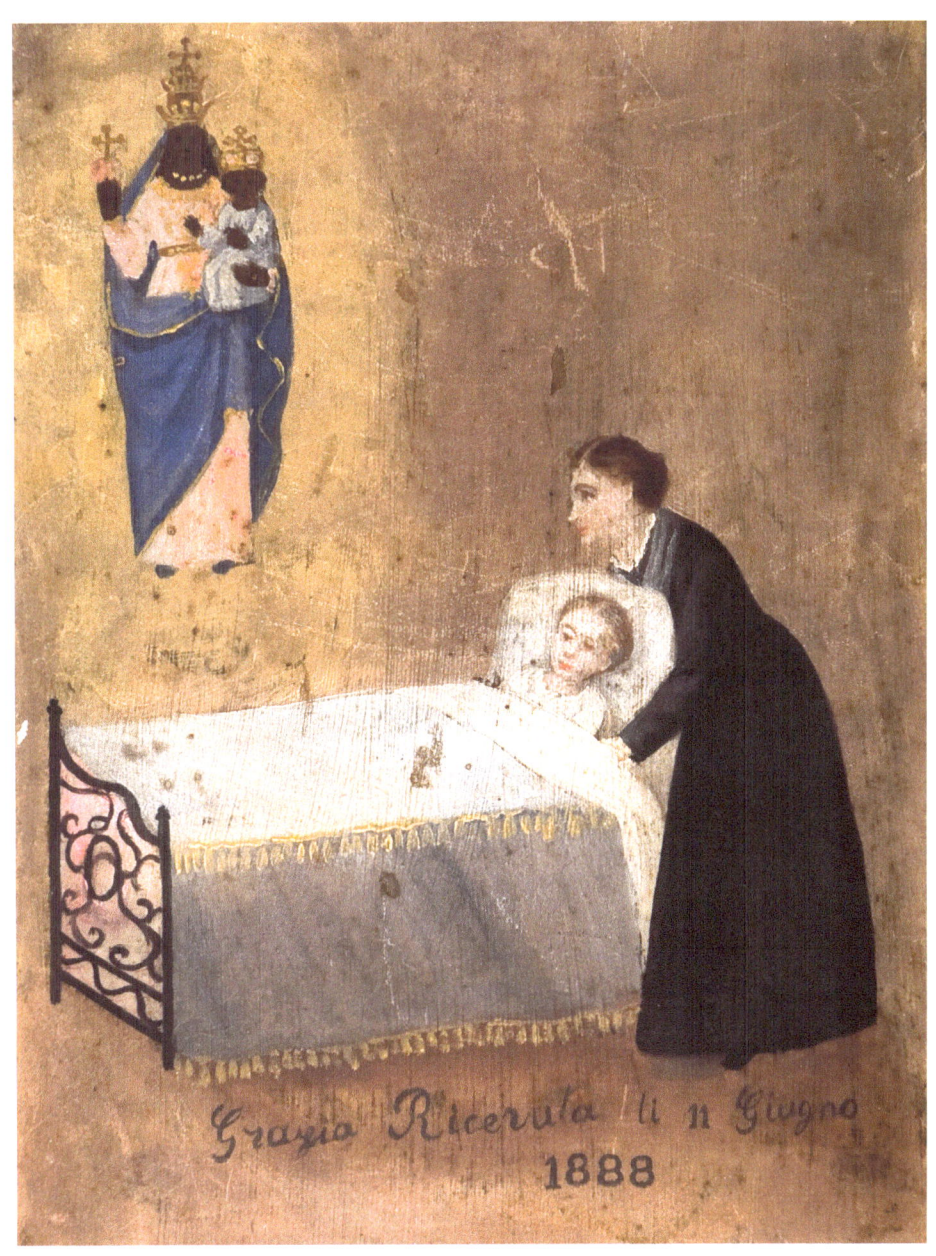

Grazia Ricevuta li n Giugno
1888

FIGURE 4

OIL ON PASTEBOARD

11¼ x 14½ INCHES (28.5 x 36.5 CM)

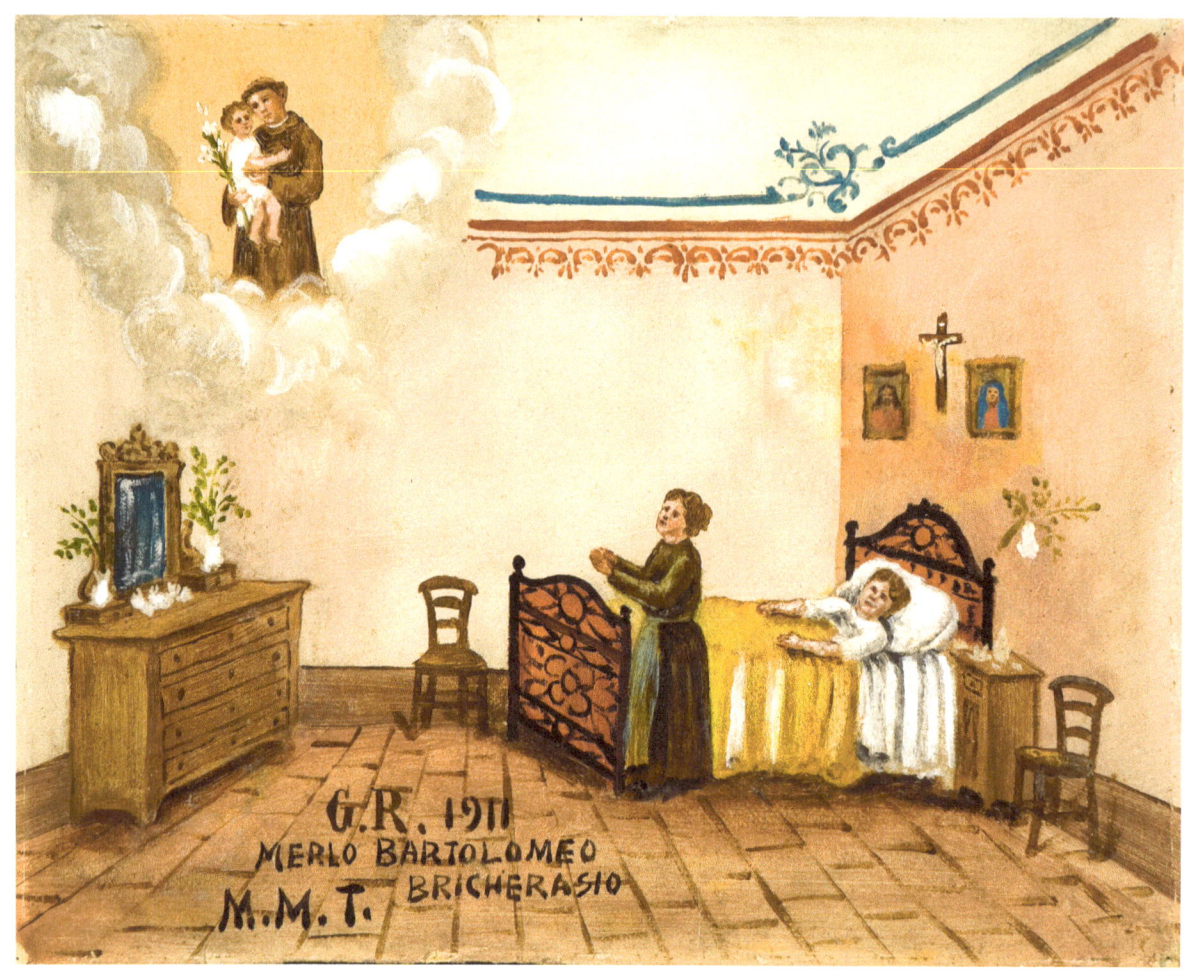

FIGURE 5

OIL ON WOOD
13¼ x 17¾ INCHES (34 x 44.5 CM)

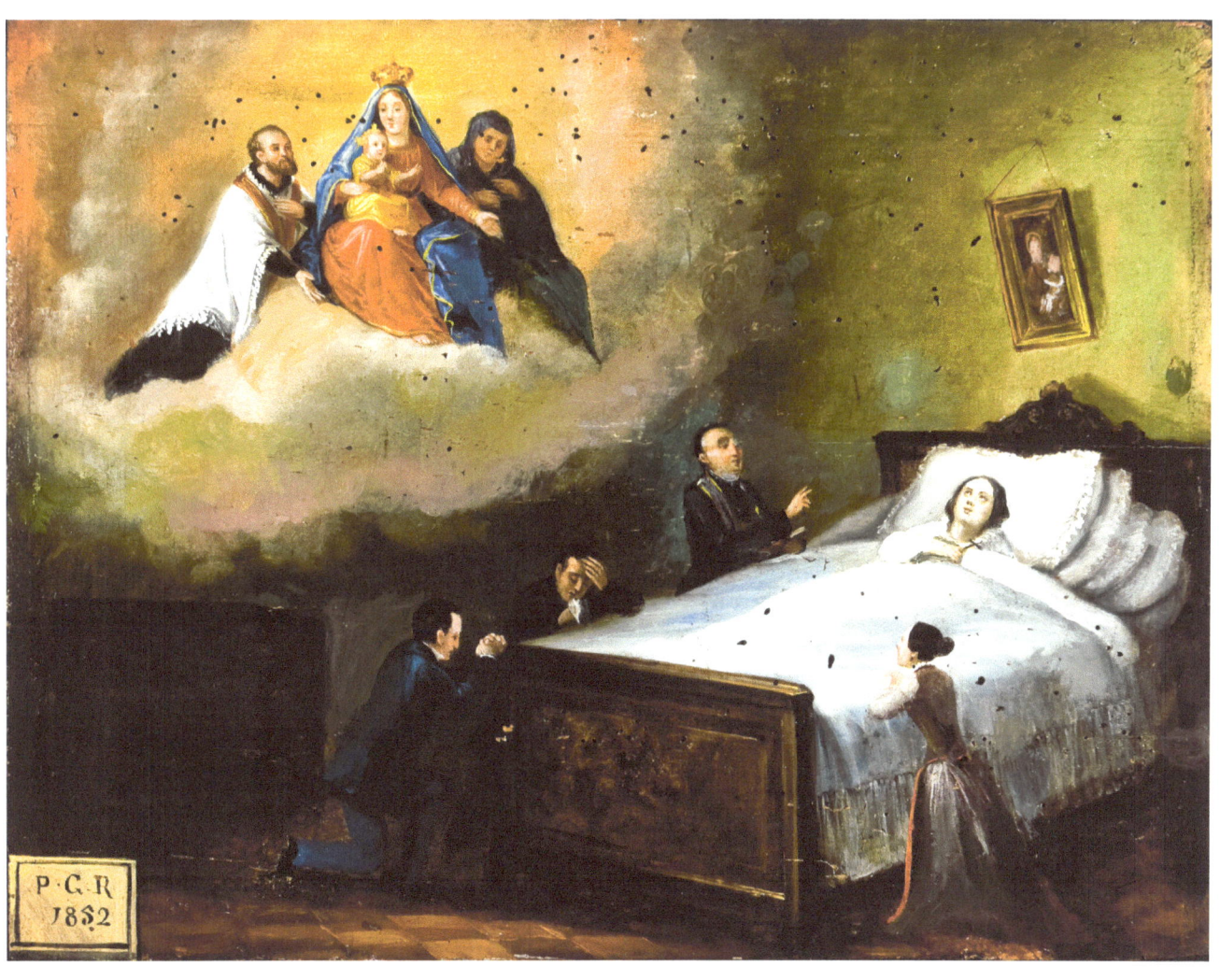

FIGURE 6

OIL ON METAL

7¾ X 11 INCHES (19 X 28 CM)

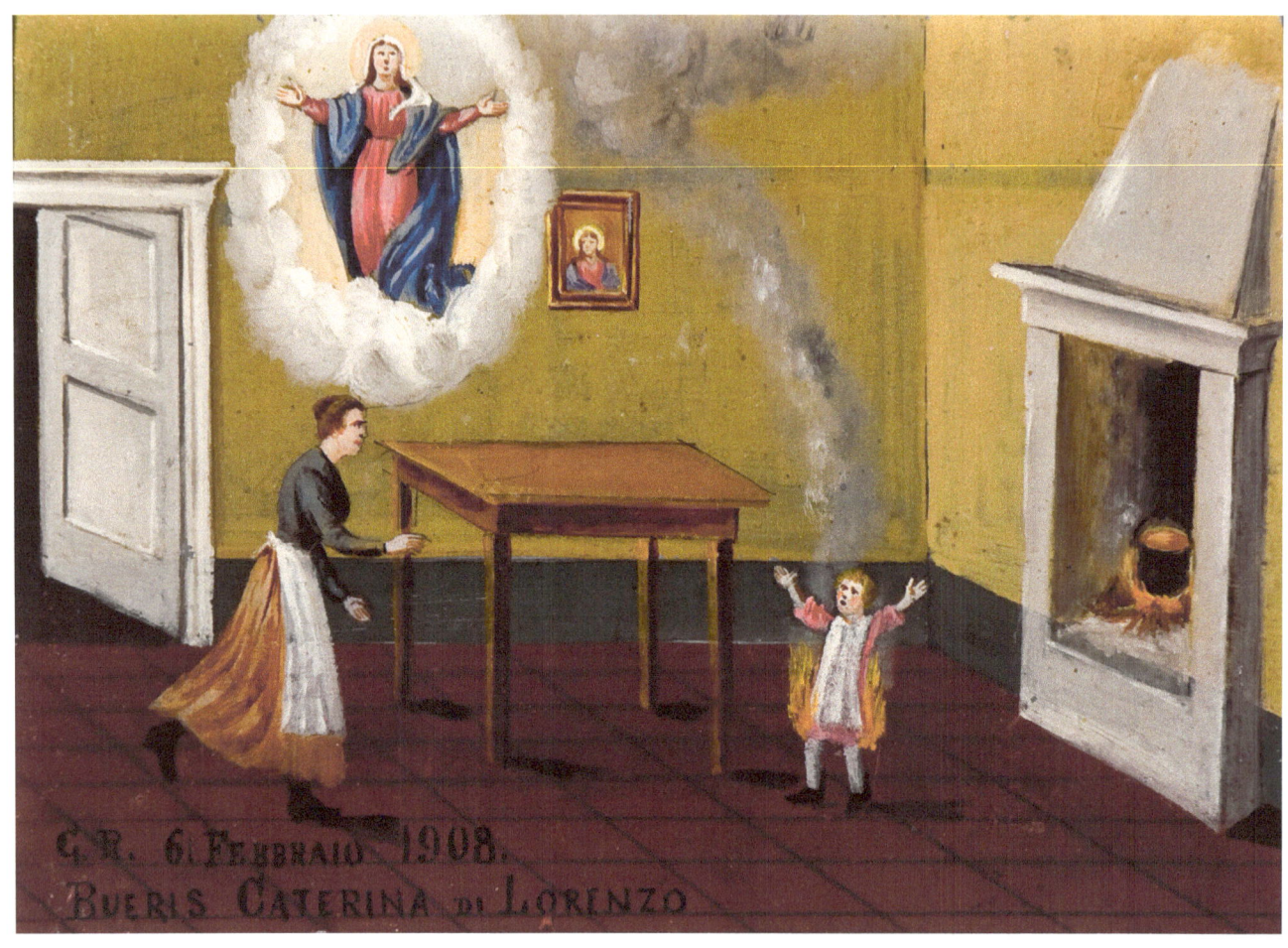

FIGURE 7

OIL ON METAL
7¾ x 10¼ INCHES (20 x 26 CM)

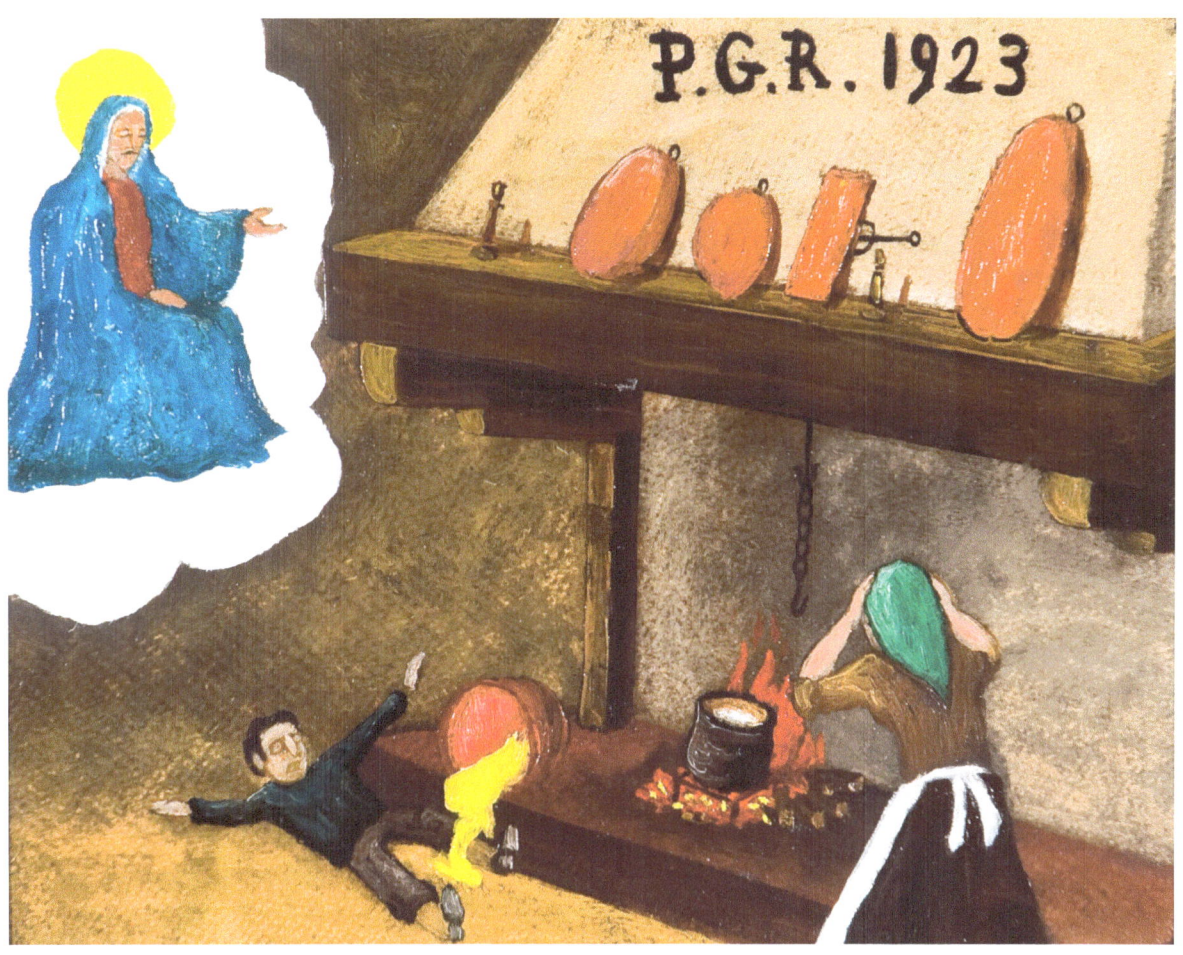

FIGURE 8

OIL ON METAL

11¾ x 8½ INCHES (29.5 x 21.5 CM)

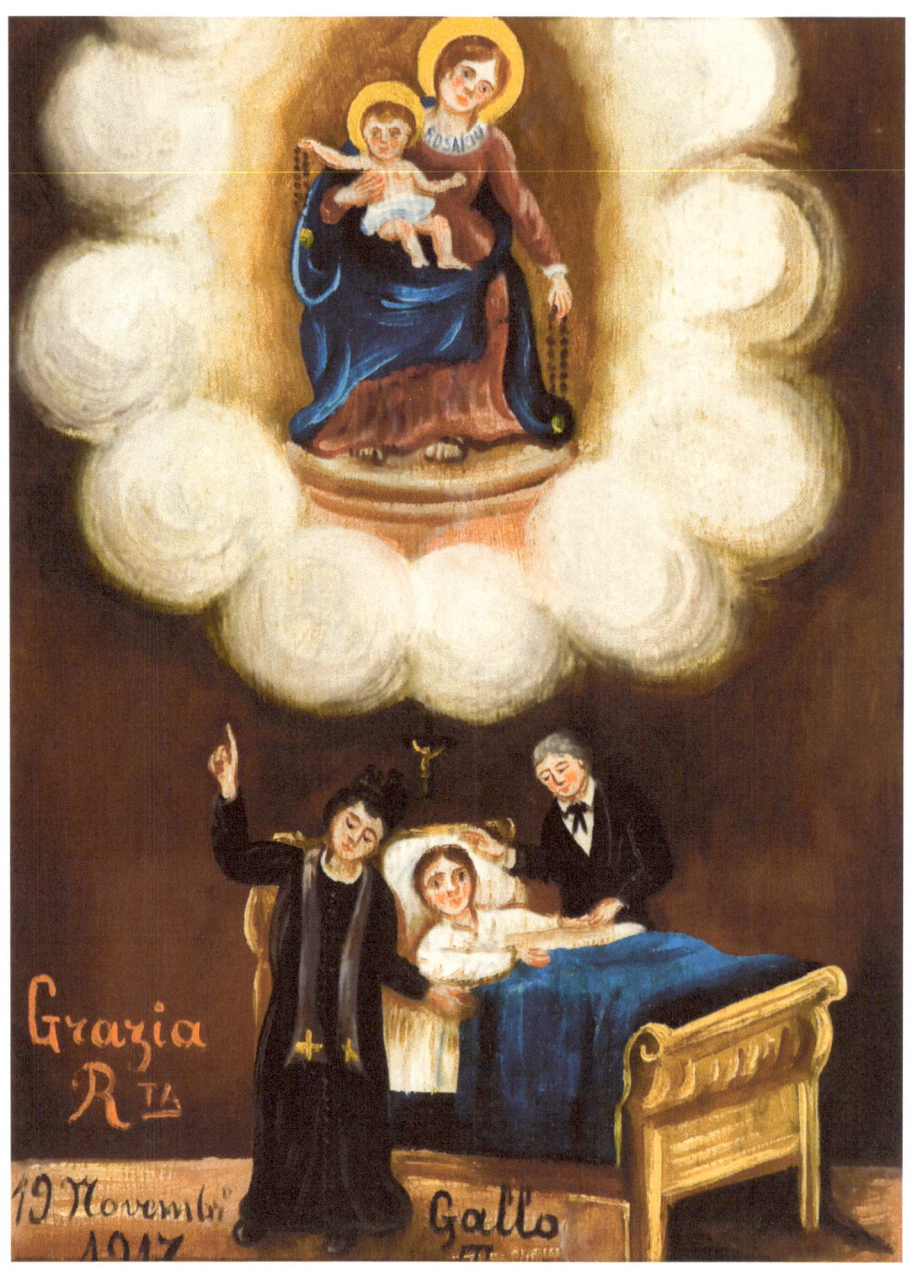

FIGURE 9

OIL ON WOOD

9 X 10¼ INCHES (23 X 26 CM)

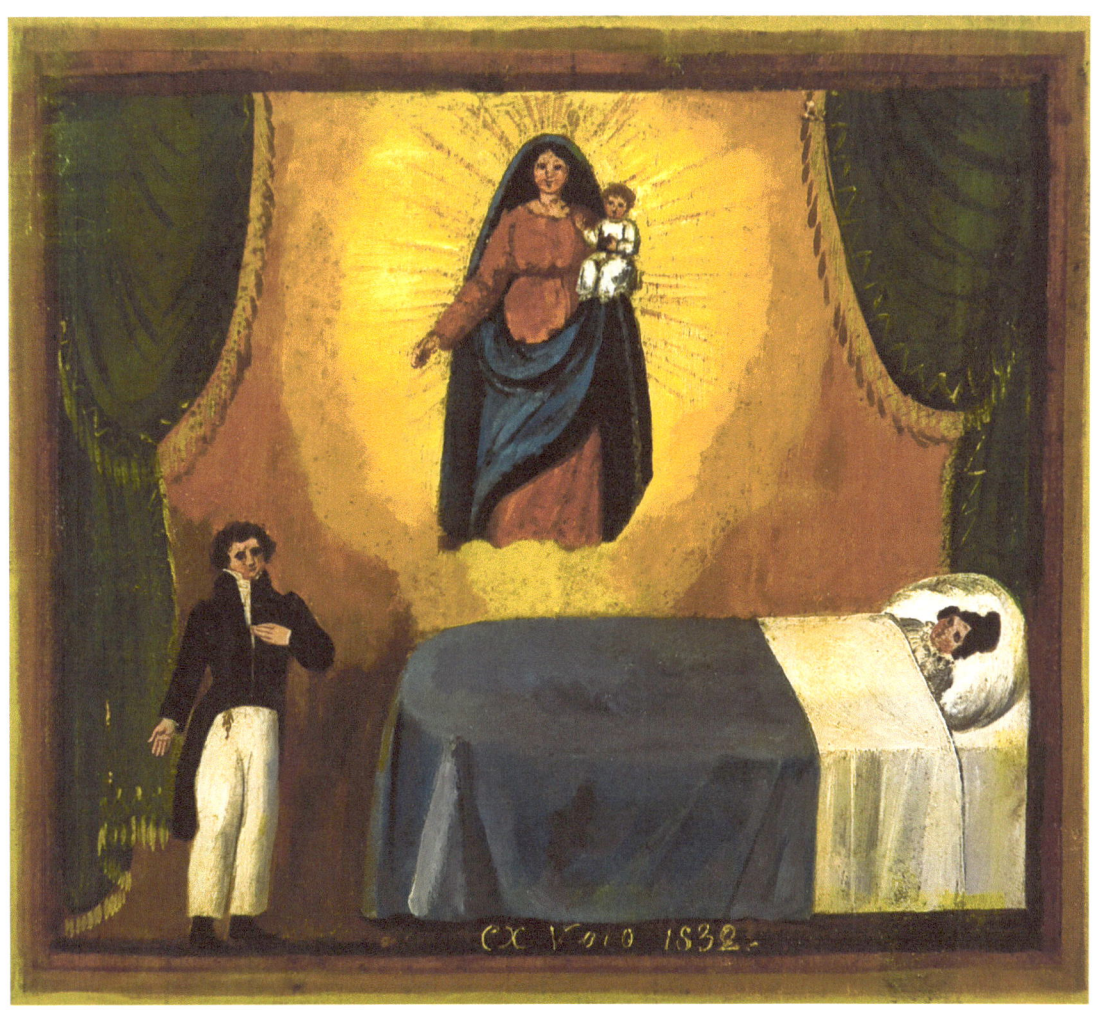

FIGURE 10

SILVERPLATE
4¼ X 3 INCHES (11 X 7.5 CM)

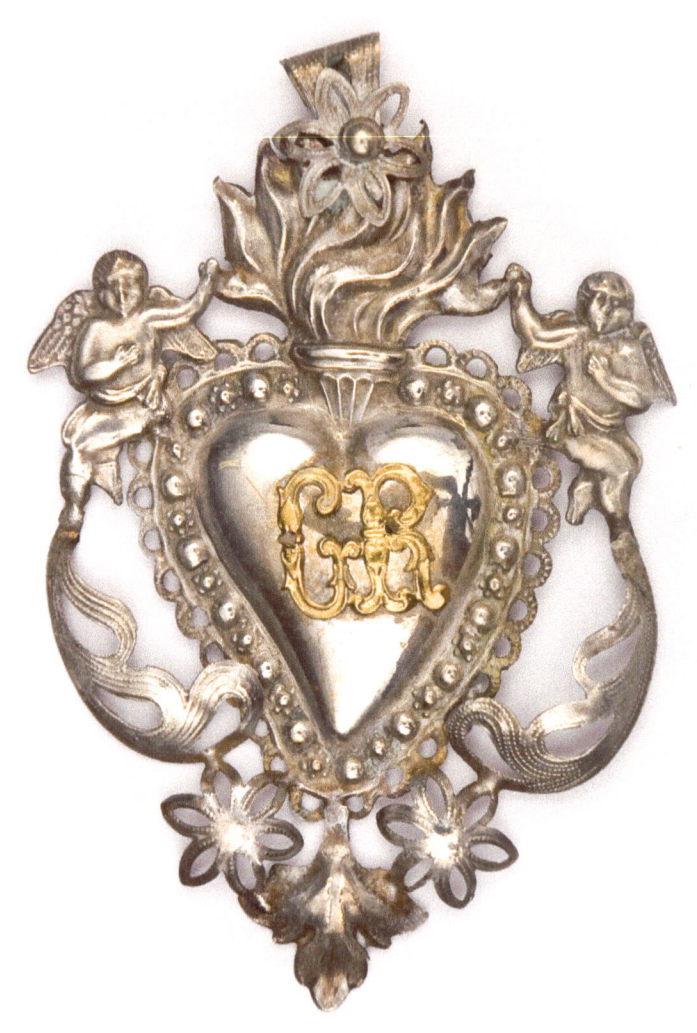

FIGURE 11

SILVERPLATE
5½ x 4¼ INCHES (14 x 11 CM)

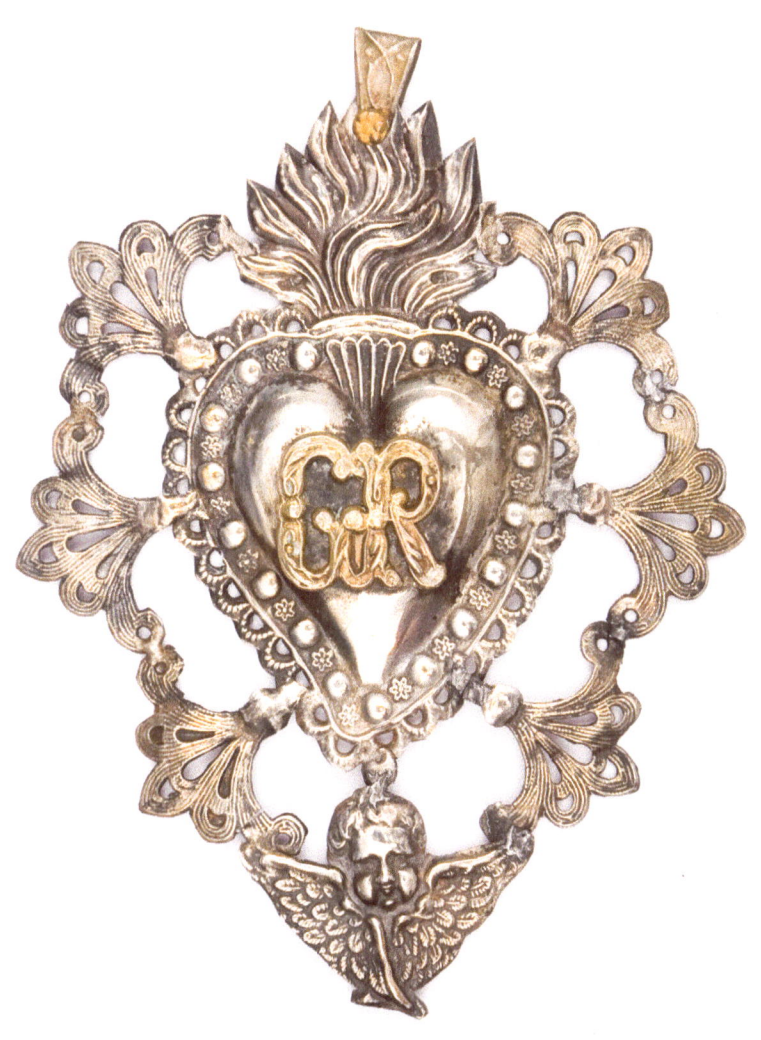

FIGURE 12

COPPER

INSCRIPTION: GR

9½ x 6 INCHES (24 x 15.5 CM)

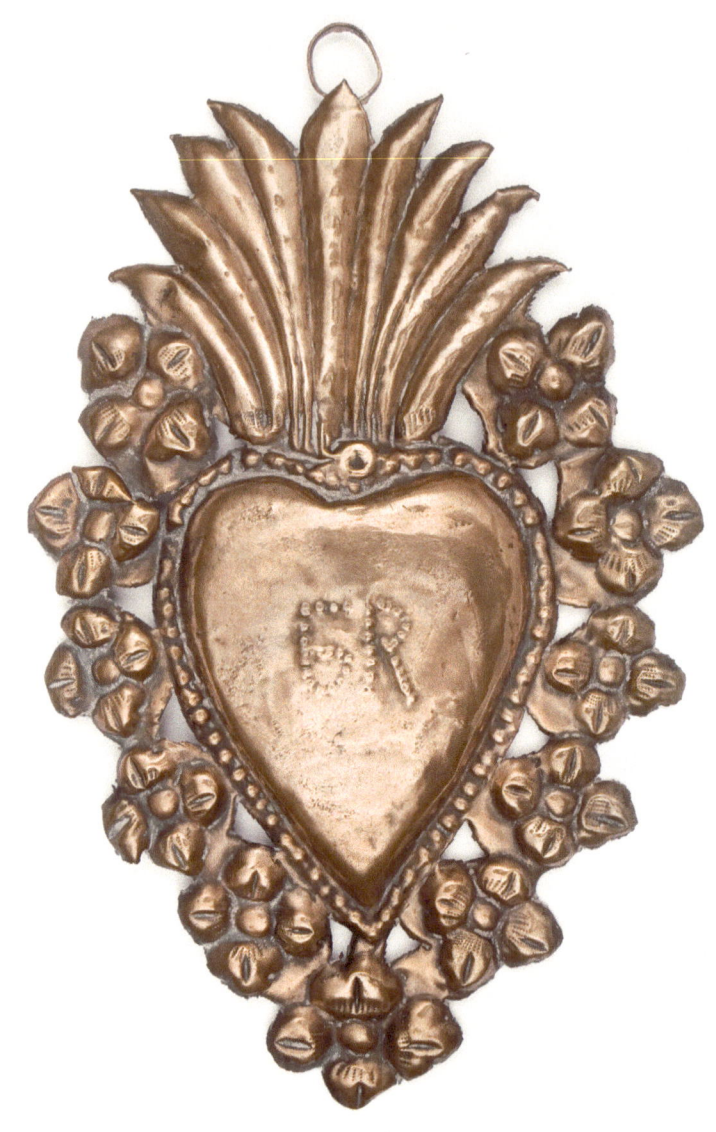

FIGURE 13

STERLING SILVER
6¾ x 4½ INCHES (17.5 x 11.5 CM)

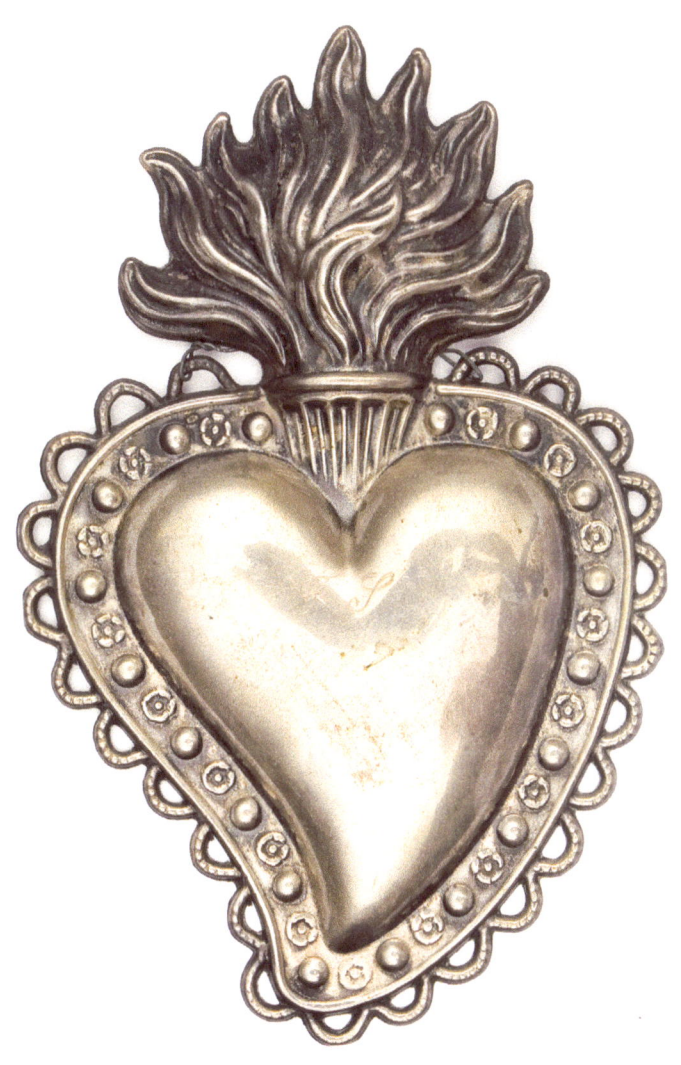

FIGURE 14

SILVERPLATE

5 X 4 INCHES (12.5 X 10 CM)

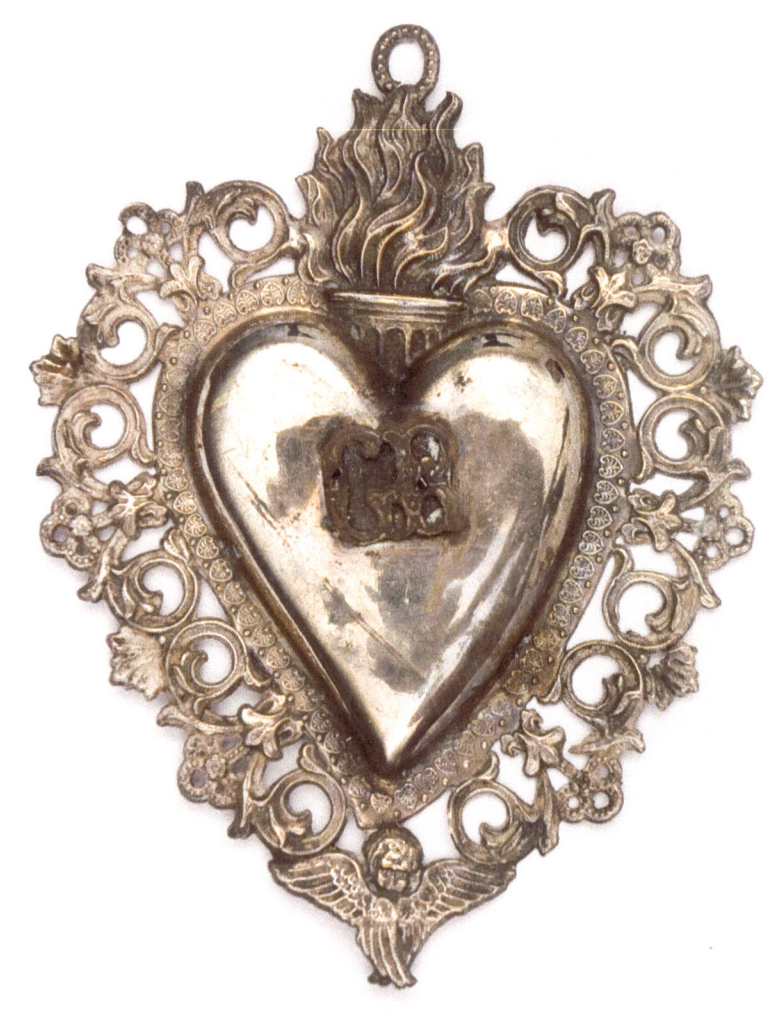

FIGURE 15

SILVERPLATE, RIBBON
7 X 5⅛ INCHES (18 X 13 CM)

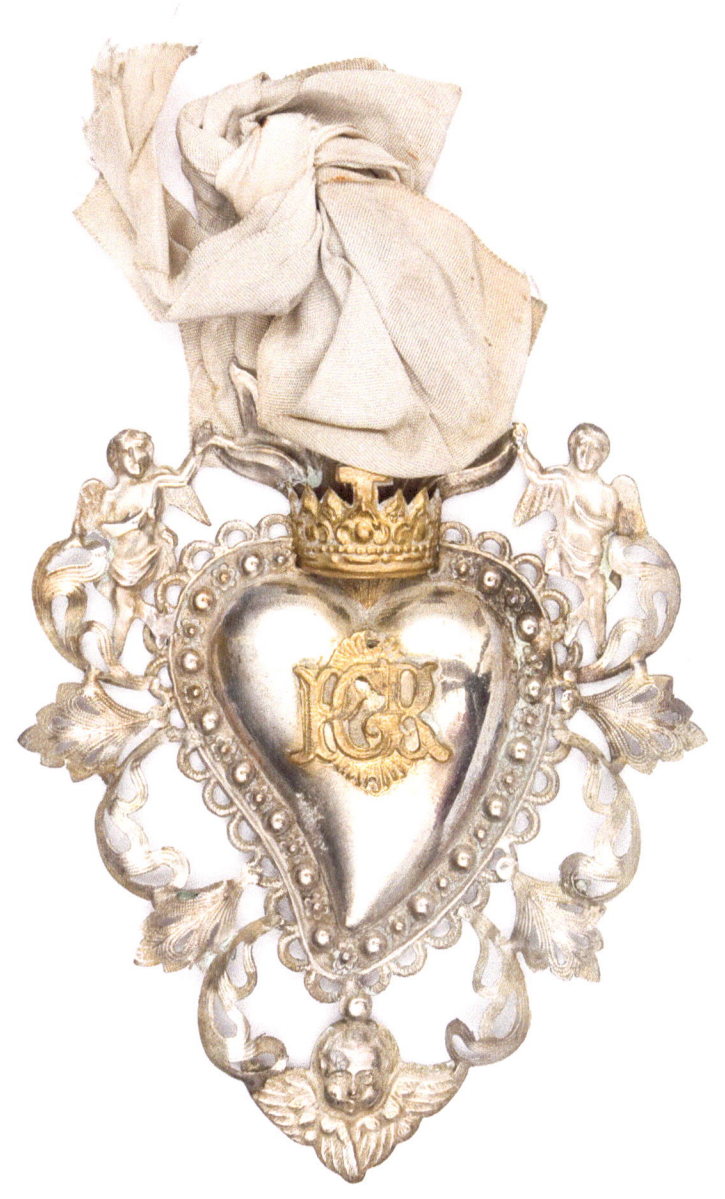

FIGURE 16

OIL ON WOOD

8 x 11½ INCHES (20 x 29.5 CM)

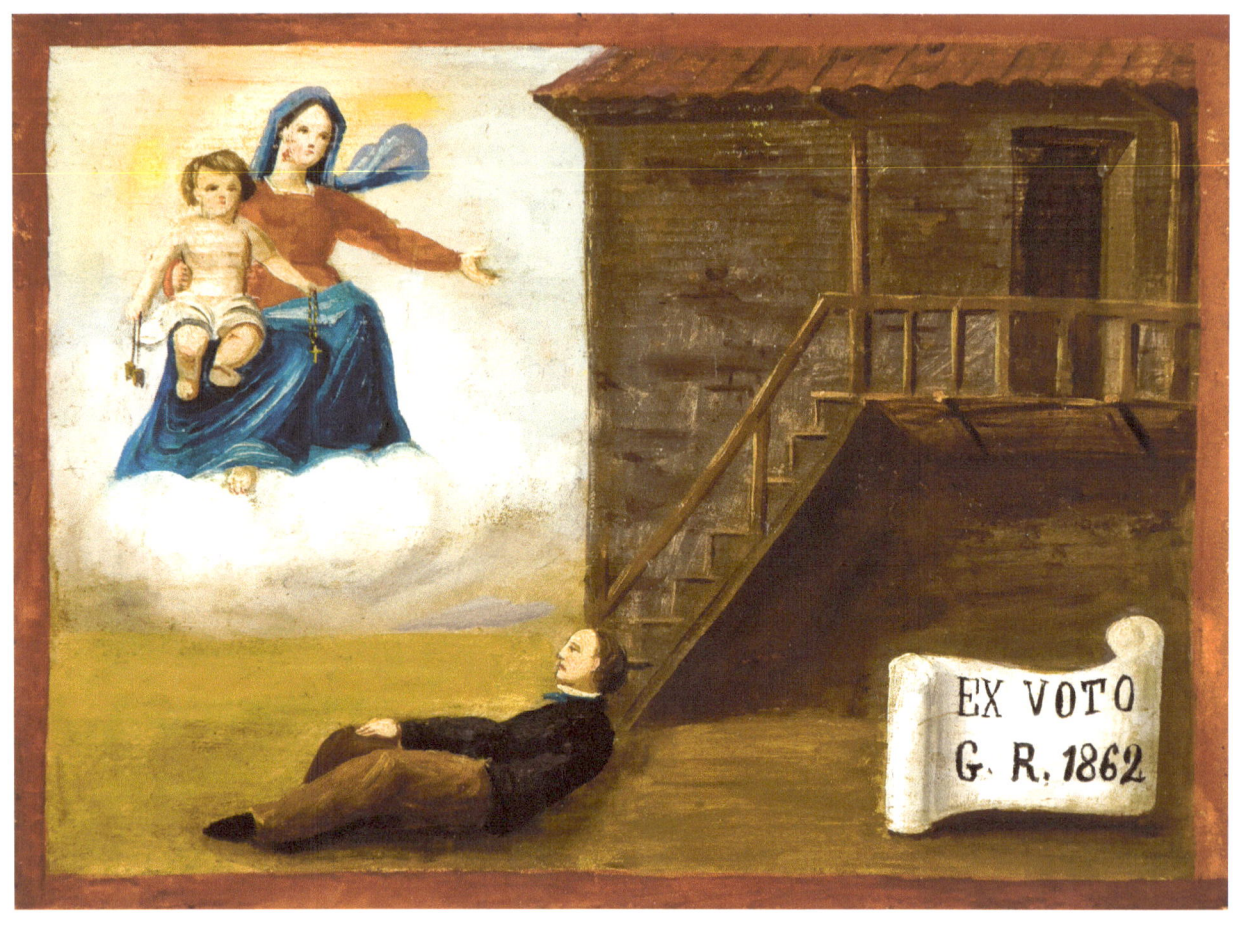

FIGURE 17

OIL ON METAL

13¾ x 9½ INCHES (34.5 x 24 CM)

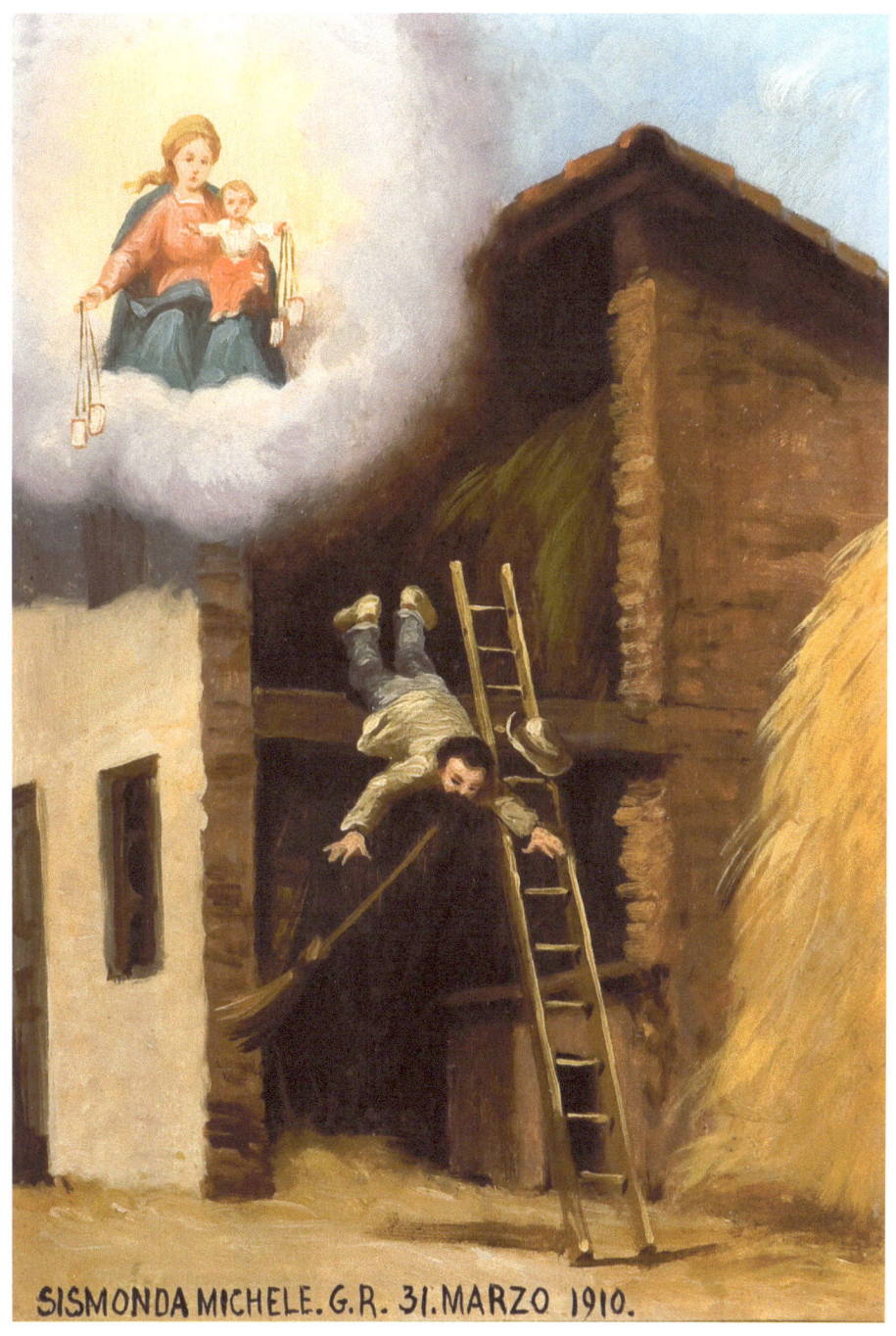

FIGURE 18

OIL ON PASTEBOARD

12¾ x 9½ INCHES (32 x 22.5 CM)

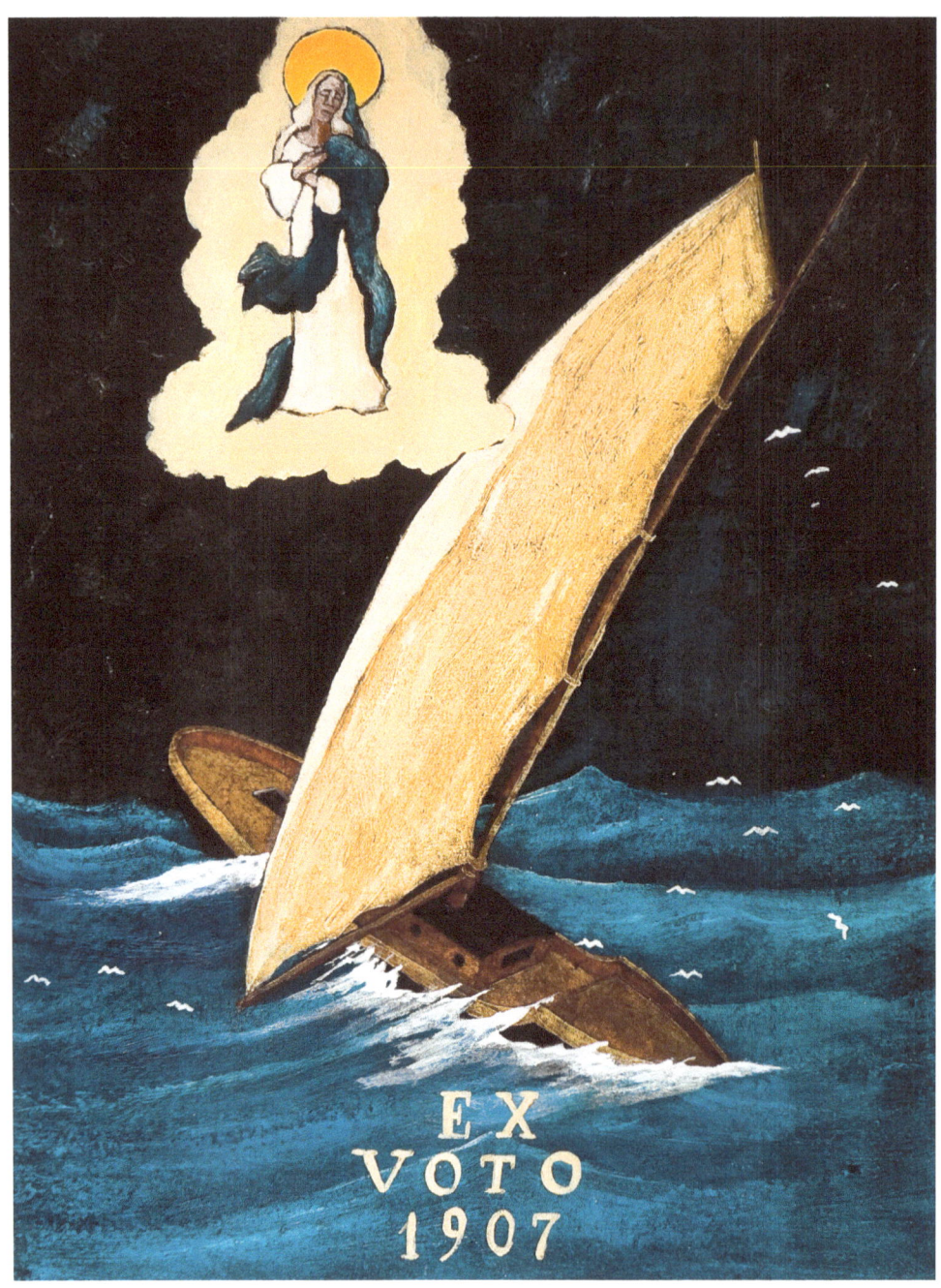

FIGURE 19

OIL ON PASTEBOARD
16 X 12 INCHES (40.5 X 30.5 CM)

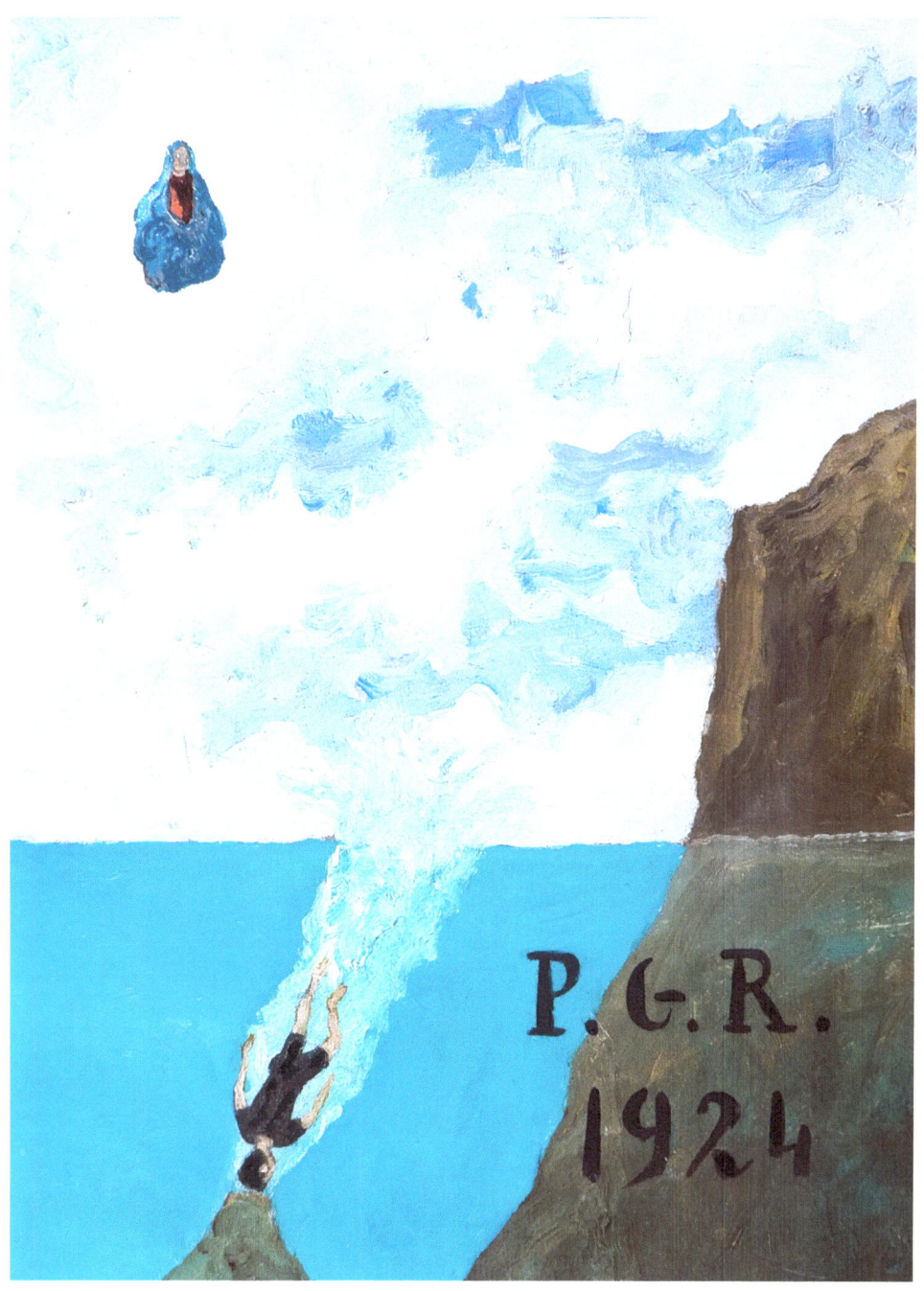

FIGURE 20

OIL ON METAL

9½ X 13¼ INCHES (24.5 X 33.5 CM)

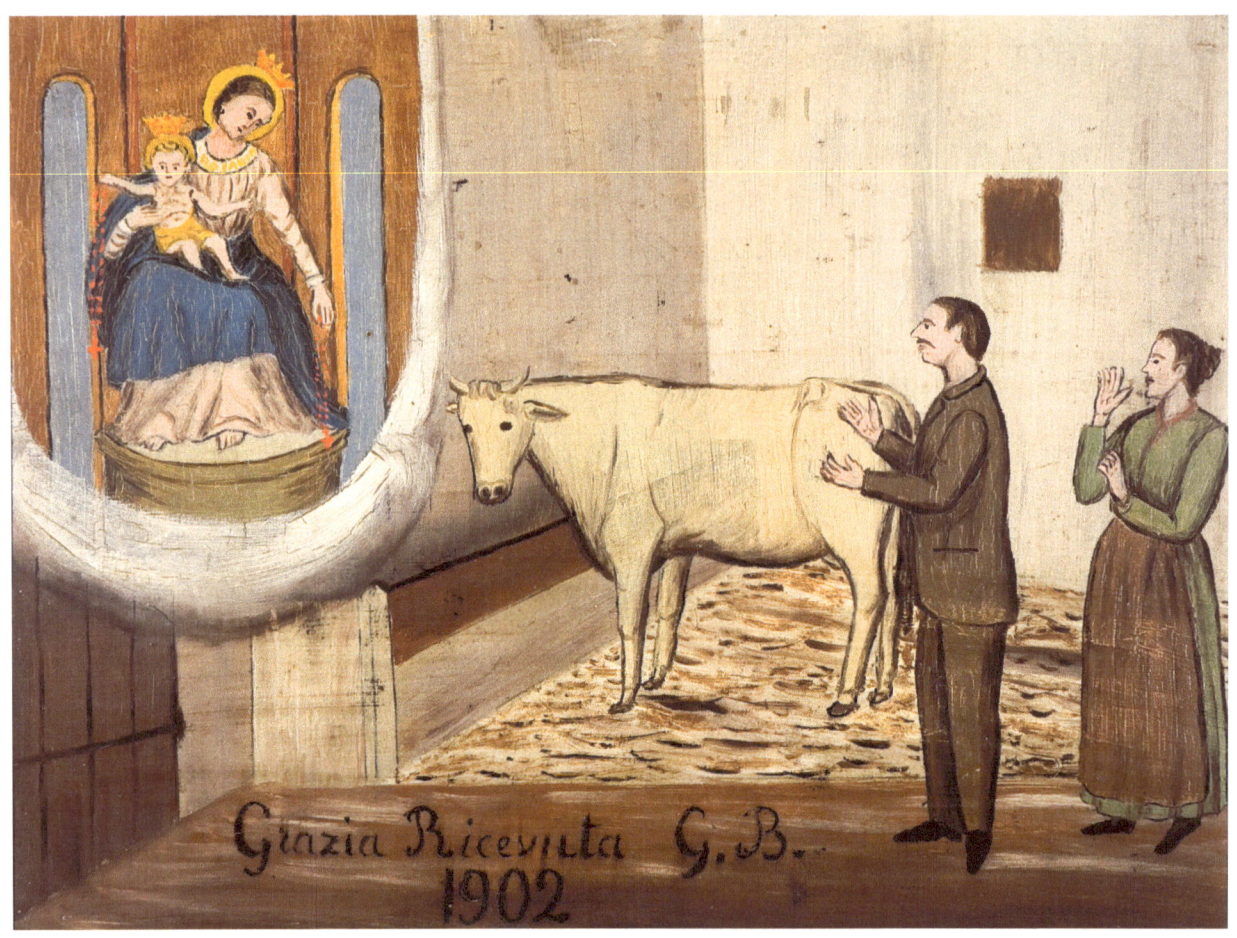

FIGURE 21

OIL ON METAL
10½ x 12¾ INCHES (26.5 x 32 CM)

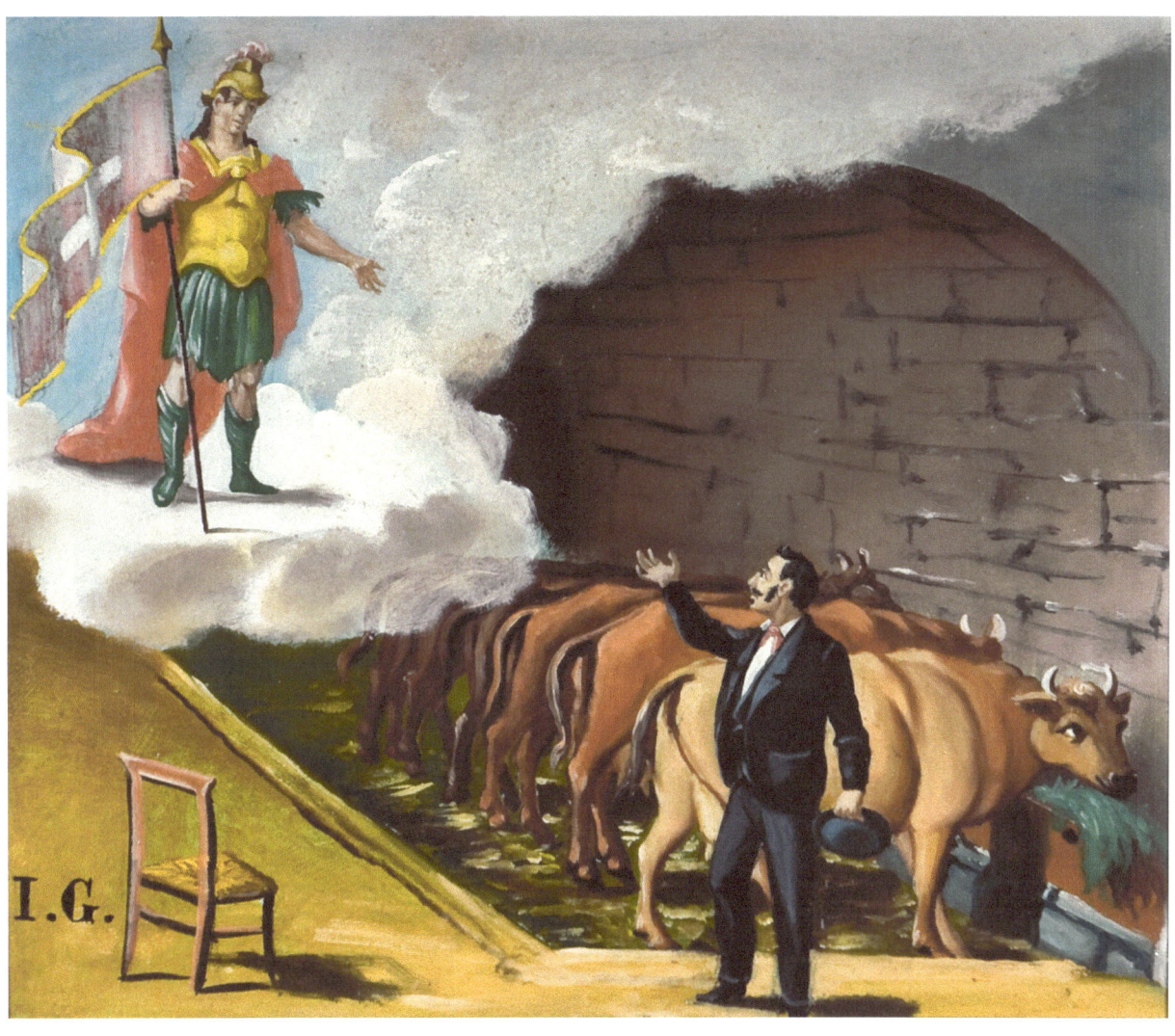

Figure 22

Oil on pasteboard

12½ x 15½ inches (32 x 39.5 cm)

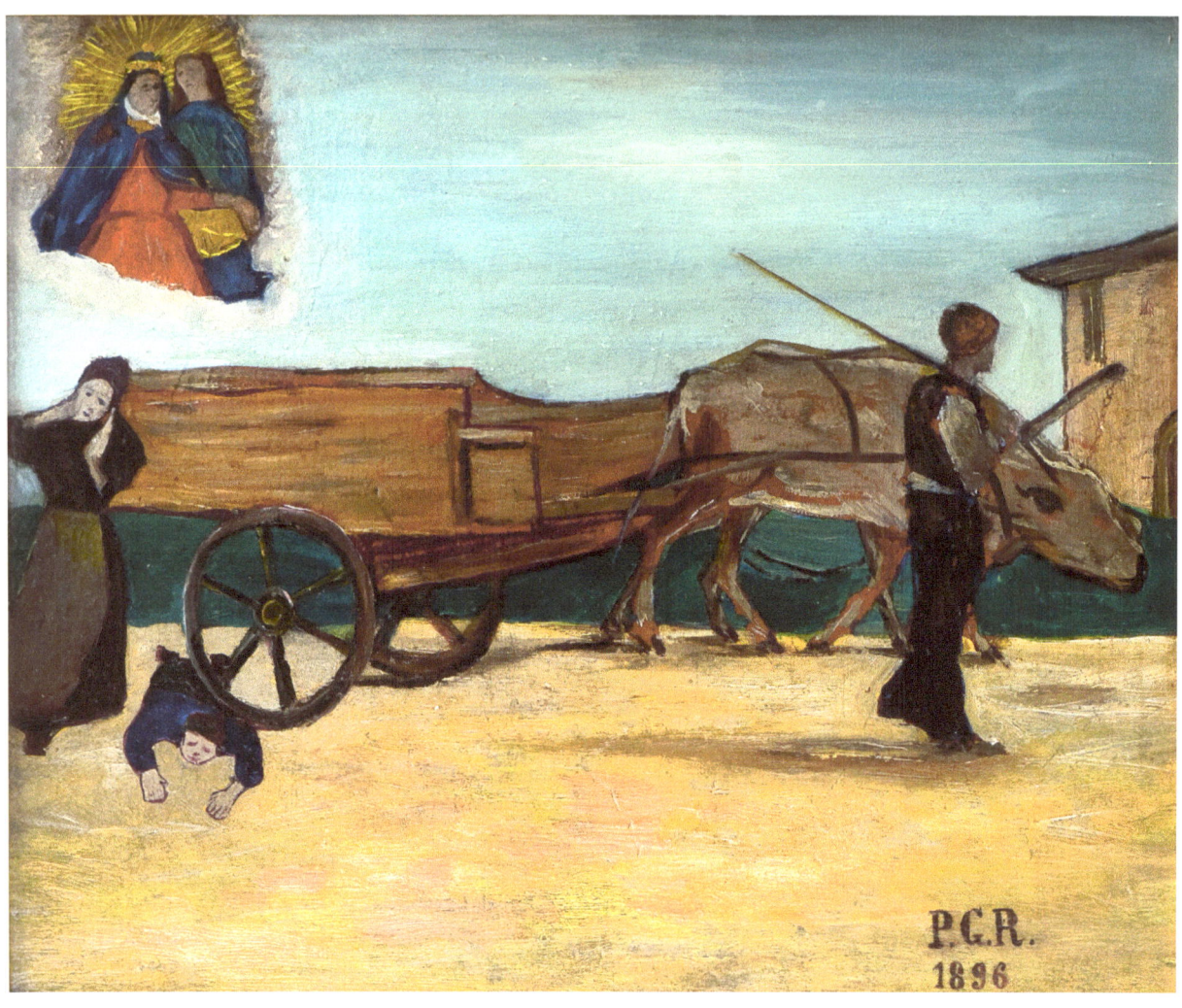

FIGURE 23

Oil on wood
10¼ x 13½ inches (26 x 34.5 cm)

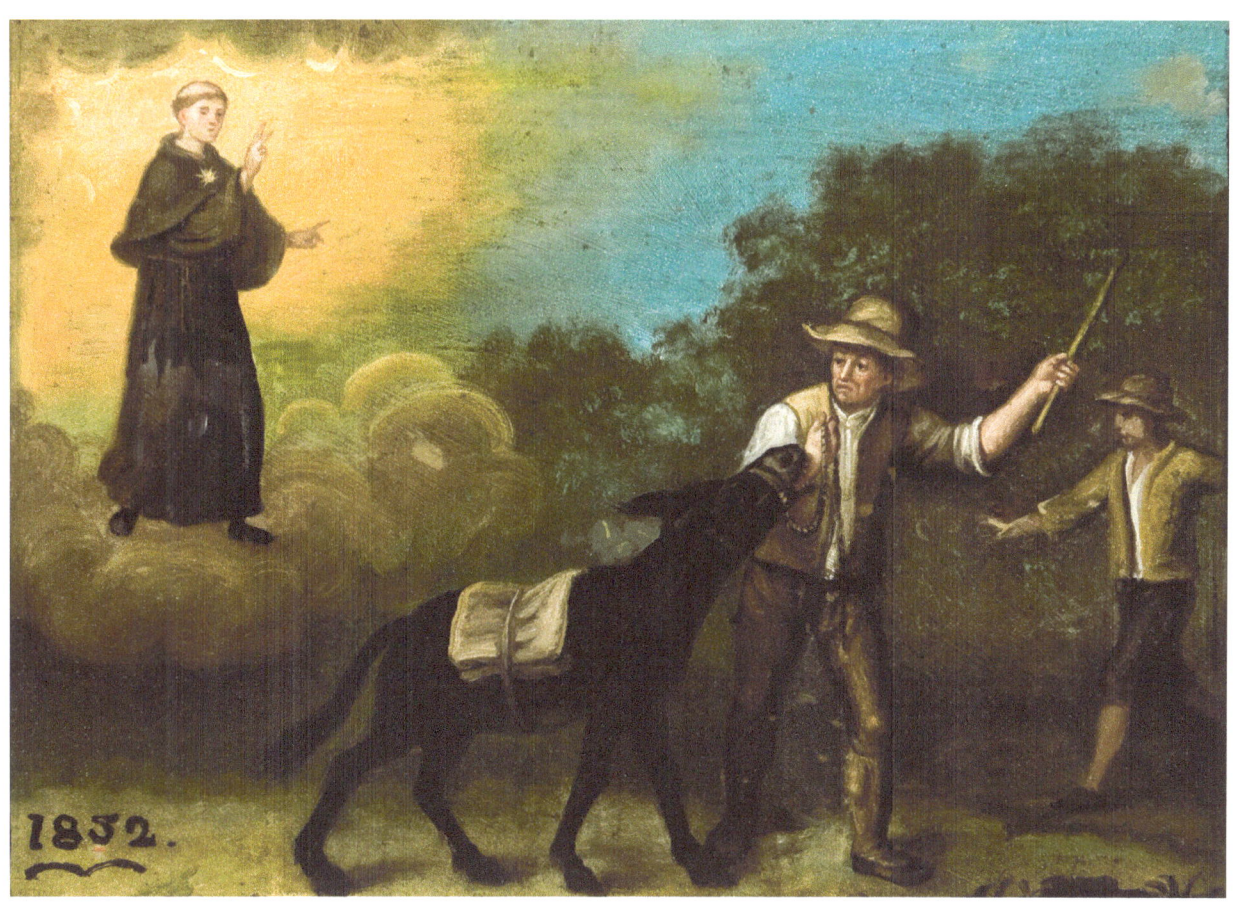

91

Figure 24

Sterling silver

7¾ x 3¼ inches (20 x 8 cm)

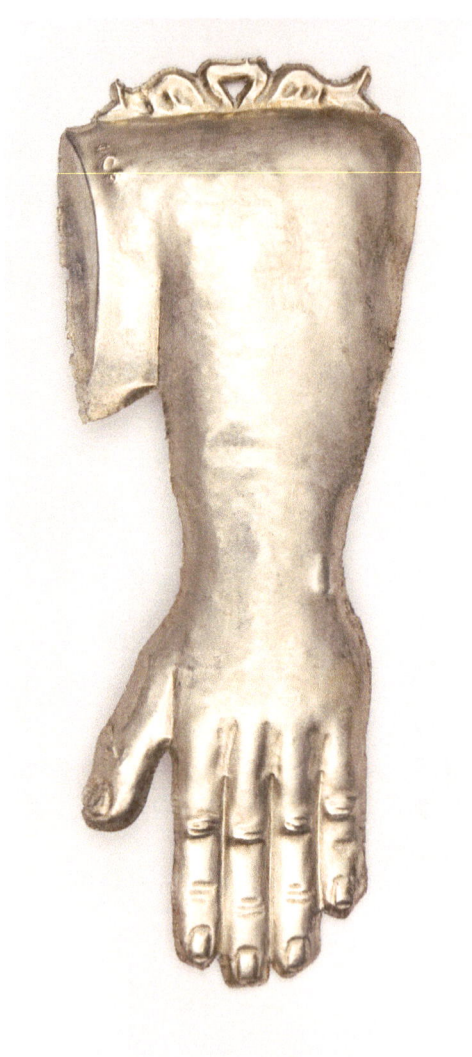

FIGURE 25

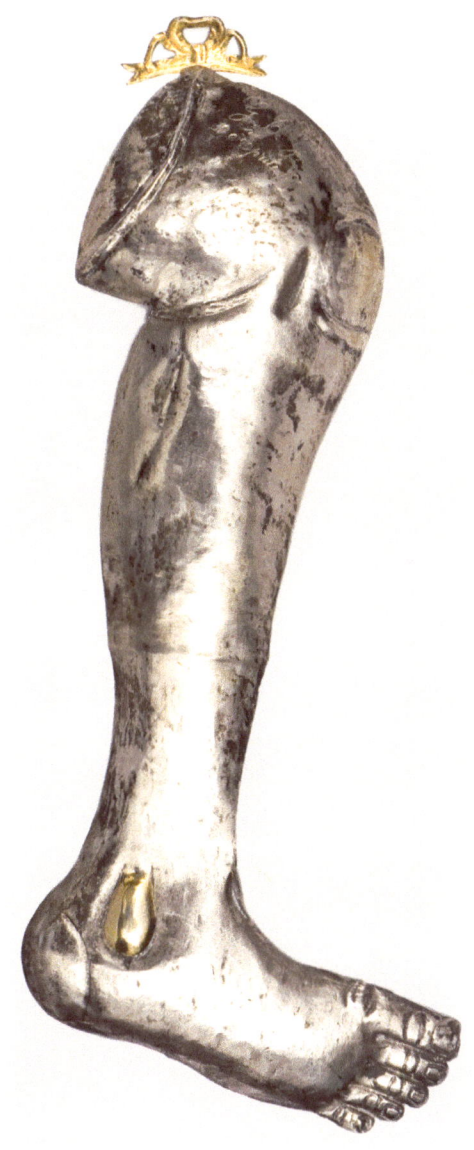

FIGURE 26

TIN

6 X 4¼ INCHES (15.5 X 10.5 CM)

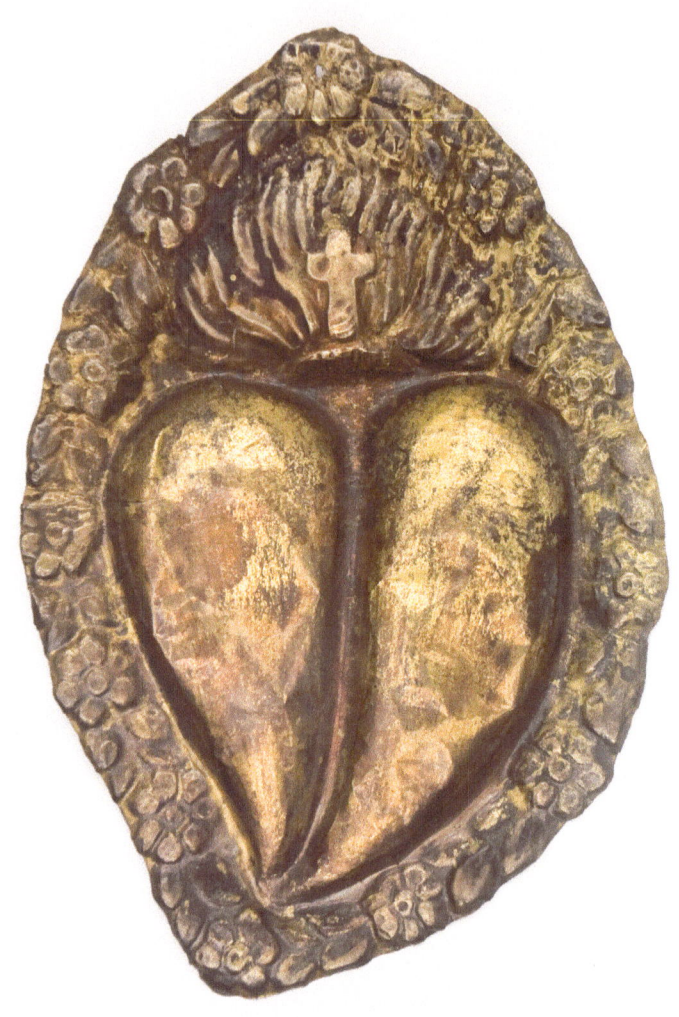

FIGURE 27

STERLING SILVER
4¼ x 3½ INCHES (11.5 x 9 CM)

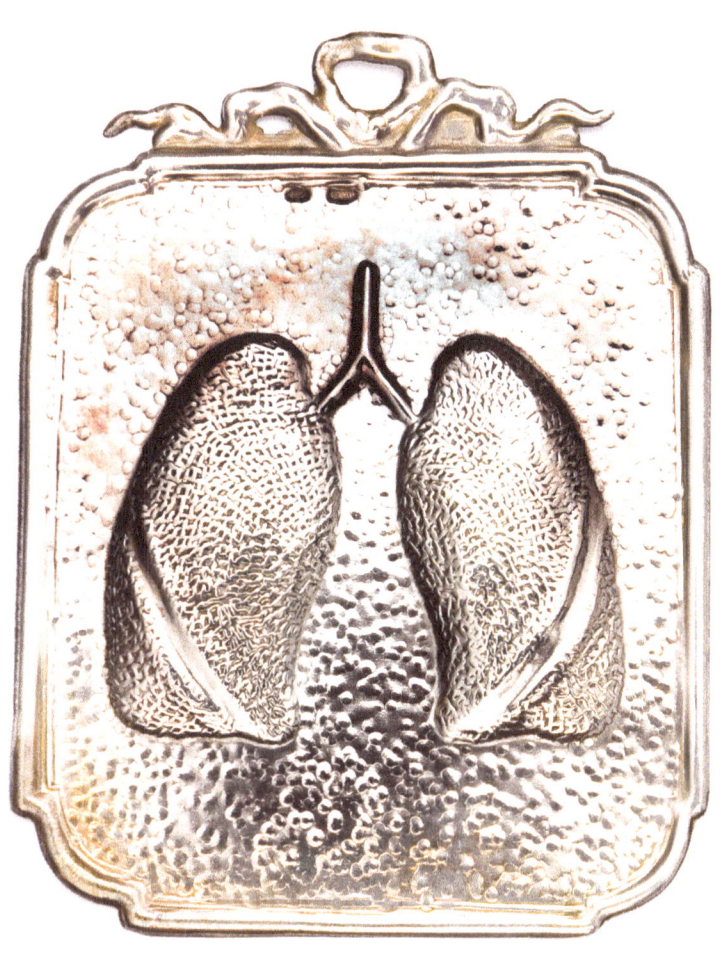

FIGURE 28

TIN

7½ x 3 INCHES (18.5 x 7.5 CM)

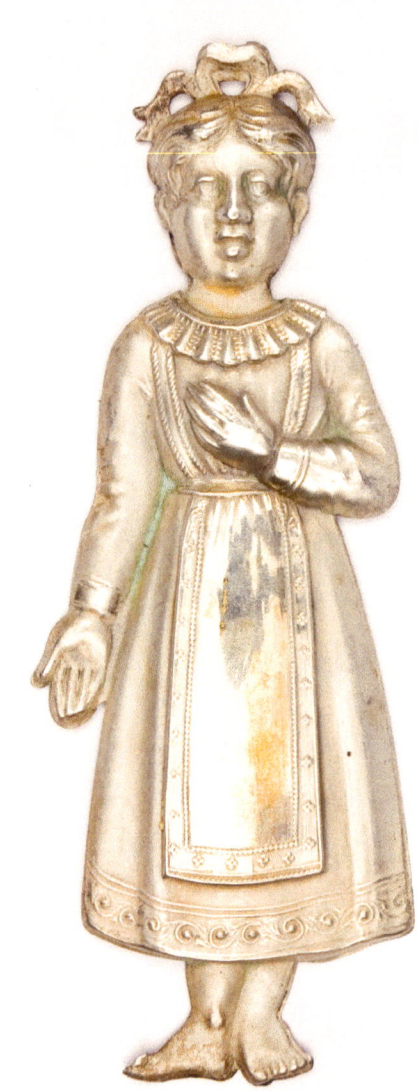

FIGURE 29

Tin

8¾ x 3 inches (22.5 x 7.5 cm)

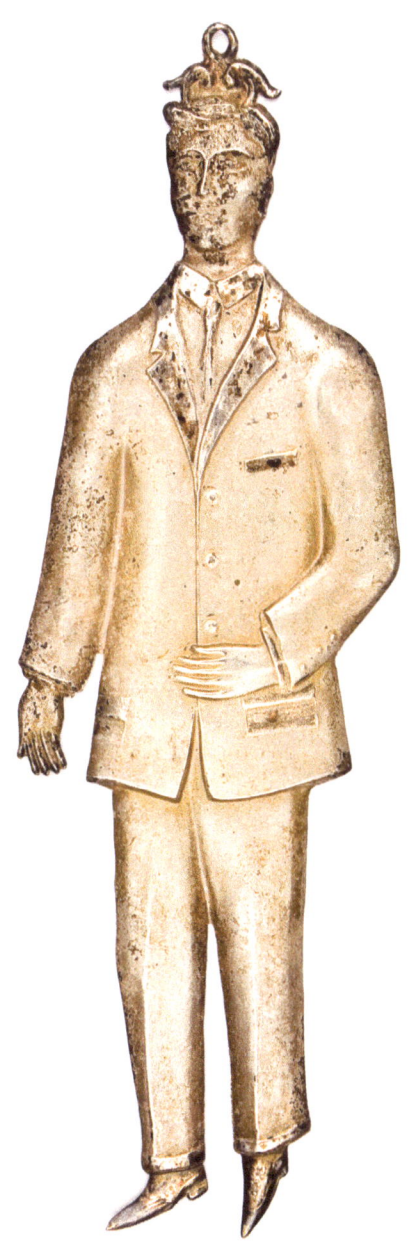

FIGURE 30

TIN

5½ X 1¾ INCHES (13.5 X 4.5 CM)

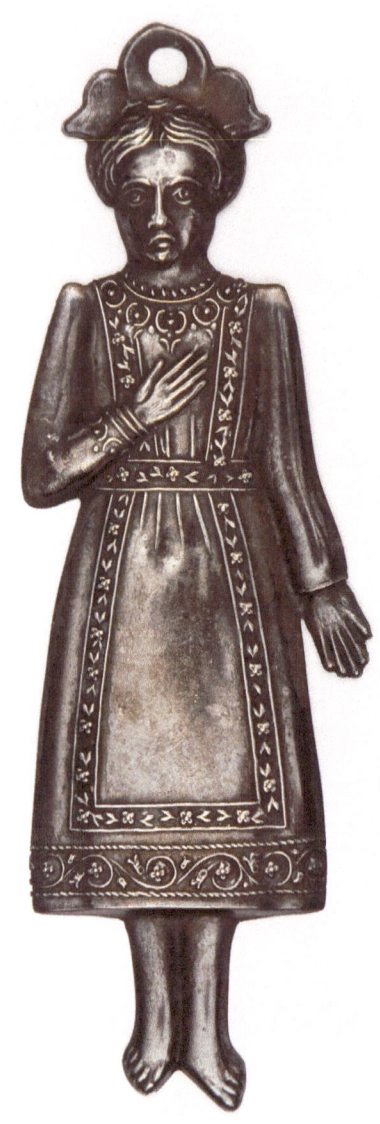

FIGURE 31

TIN
6½ x 2¾ INCHES (16.5 X 6.5 CM)

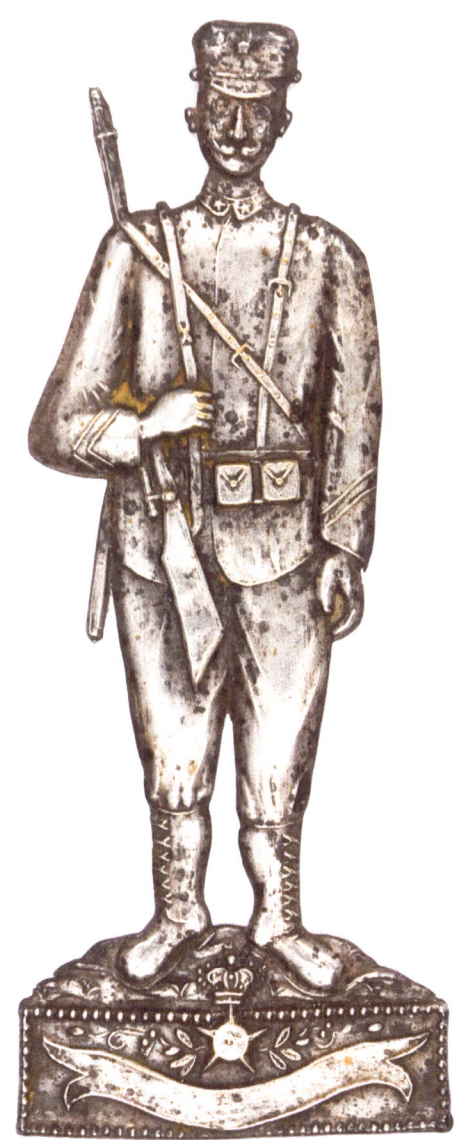

FIGURE 32

OIL ON WOOD
12 X 16¾ INCHES (30.5 X 43 CM)

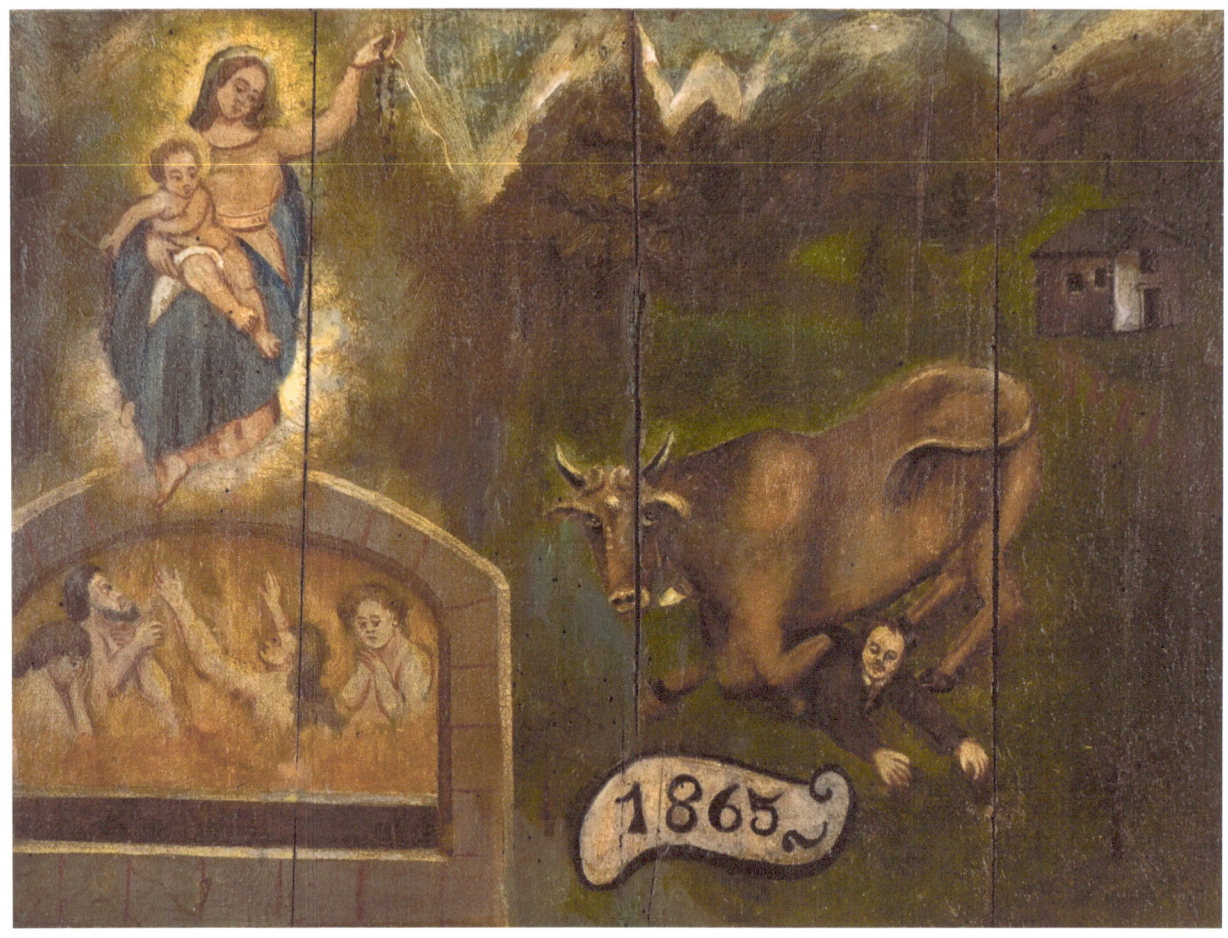

FIGURE 33

OIL ON METAL
9½ X 13¼ INCHES (24 X 33.5 CM)

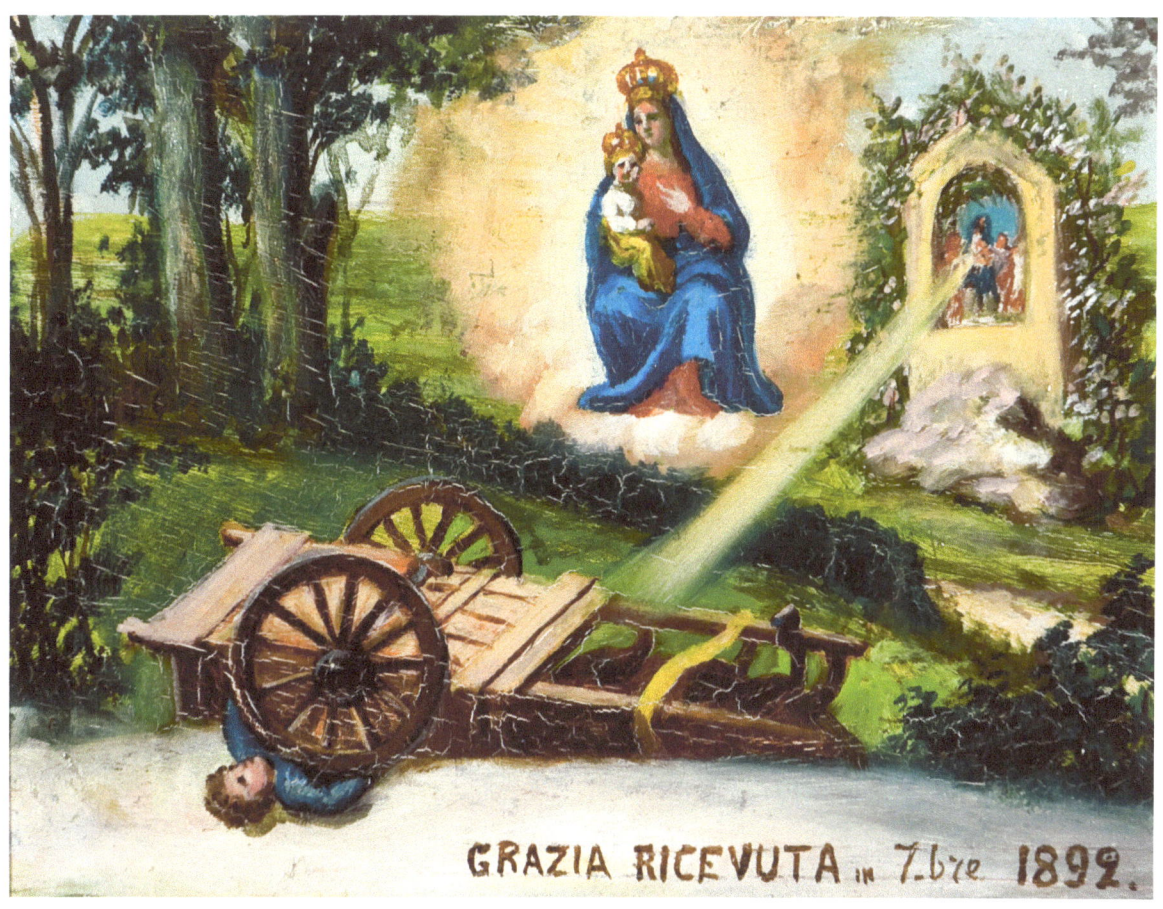

FIGURE 34

OIL ON METAL

11½ X 16 INCHES (29.5 X 40.5 CM)

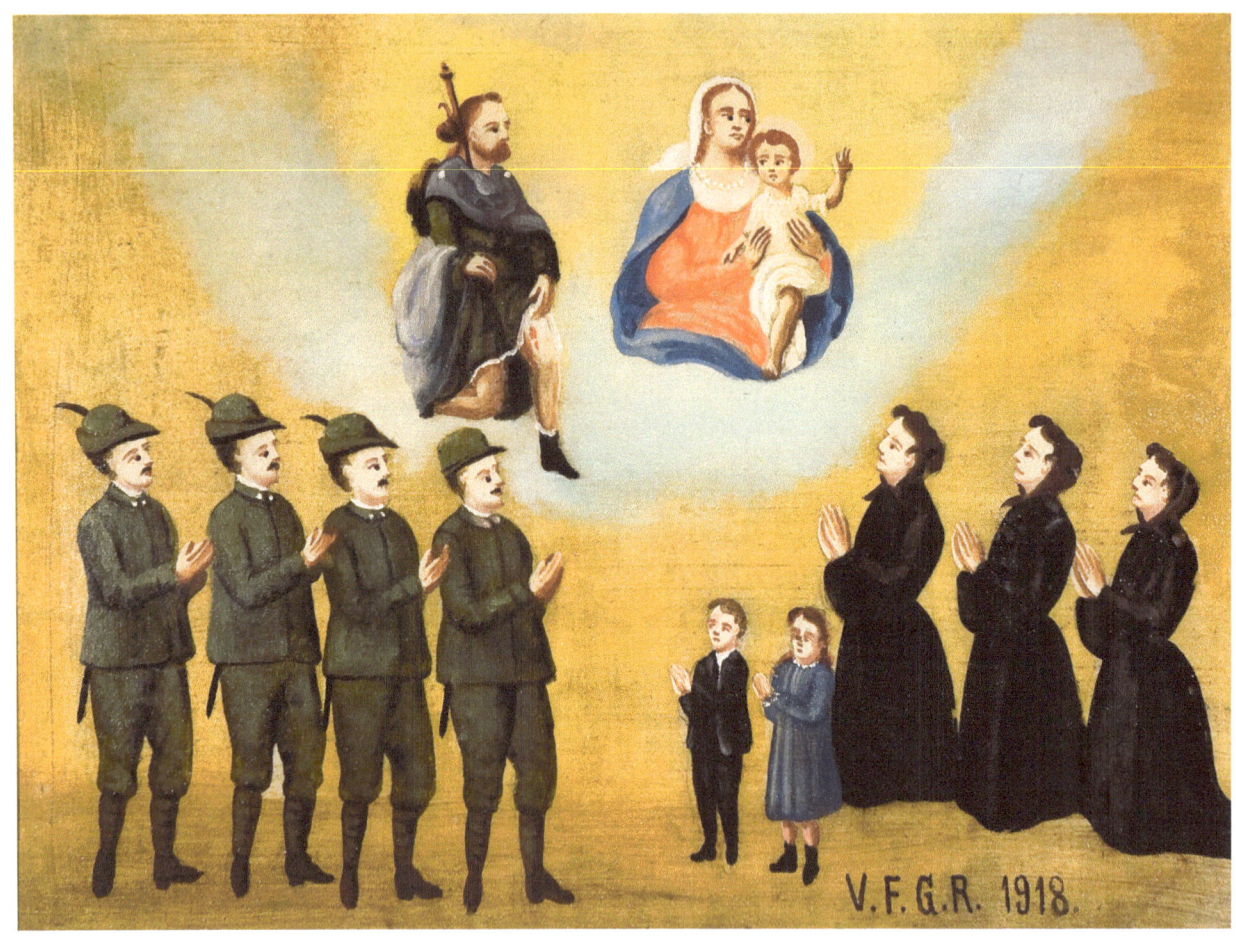

FIGURE 35

OIL ON CANVAS
28¼ X 38 INCHES (71.5 X 97 CM)

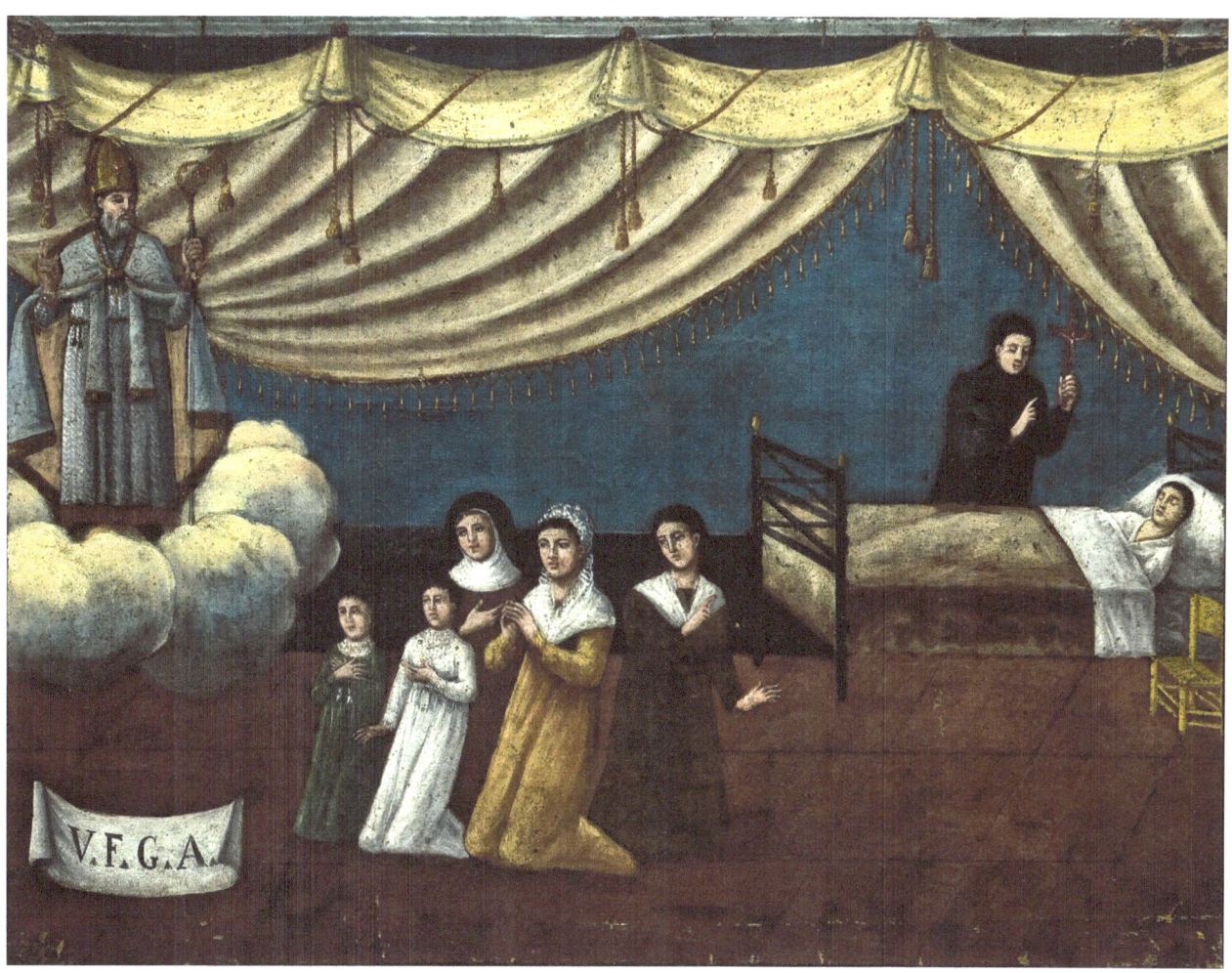

FIGURE 36

OIL ON METAL

9½ X 13¾ INCHES (24 X 35 CM)

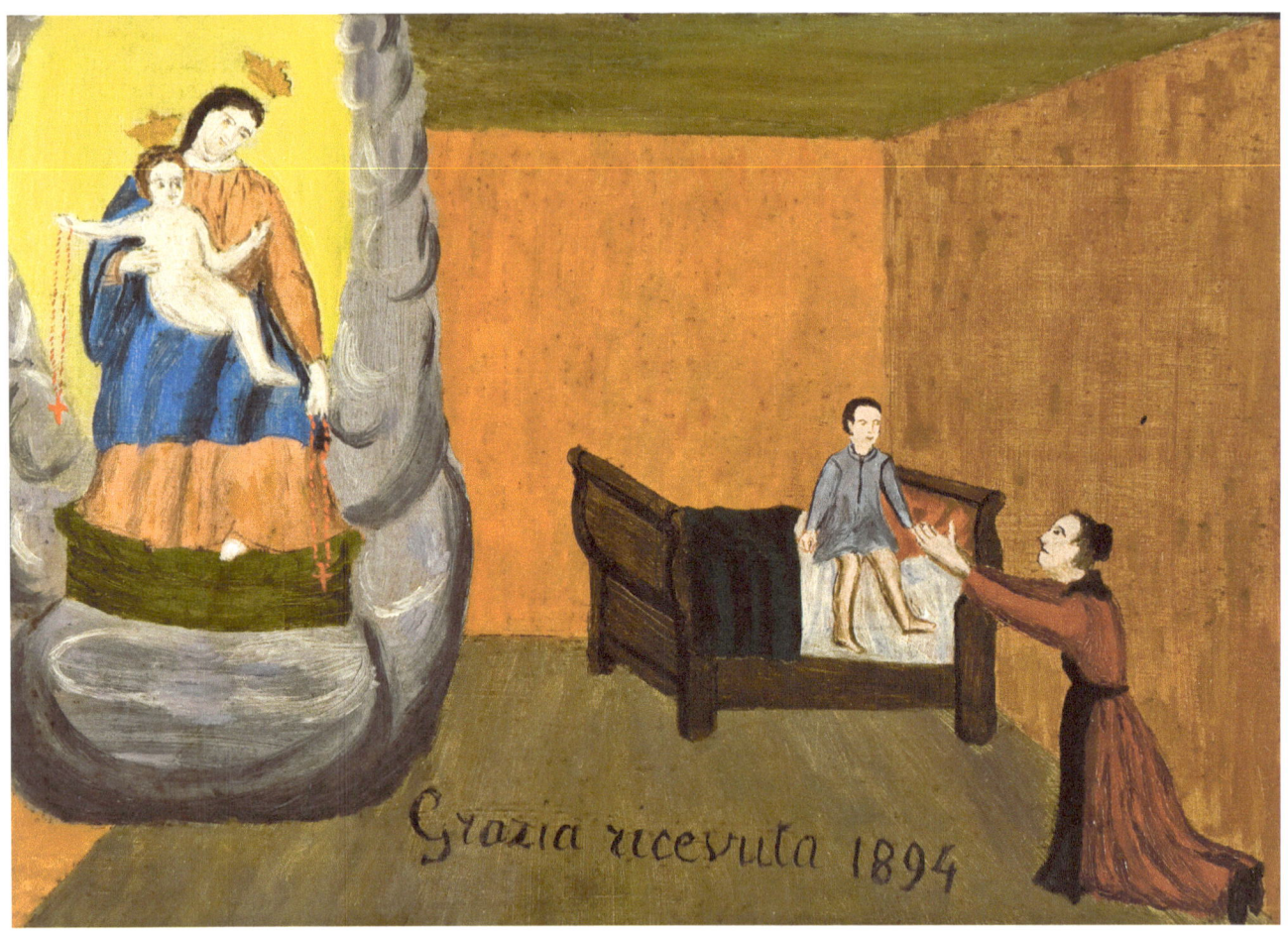

FIGURE 37

OIL ON WOOD
11 X 11¾ INCHES (28 X 29.5 CM)

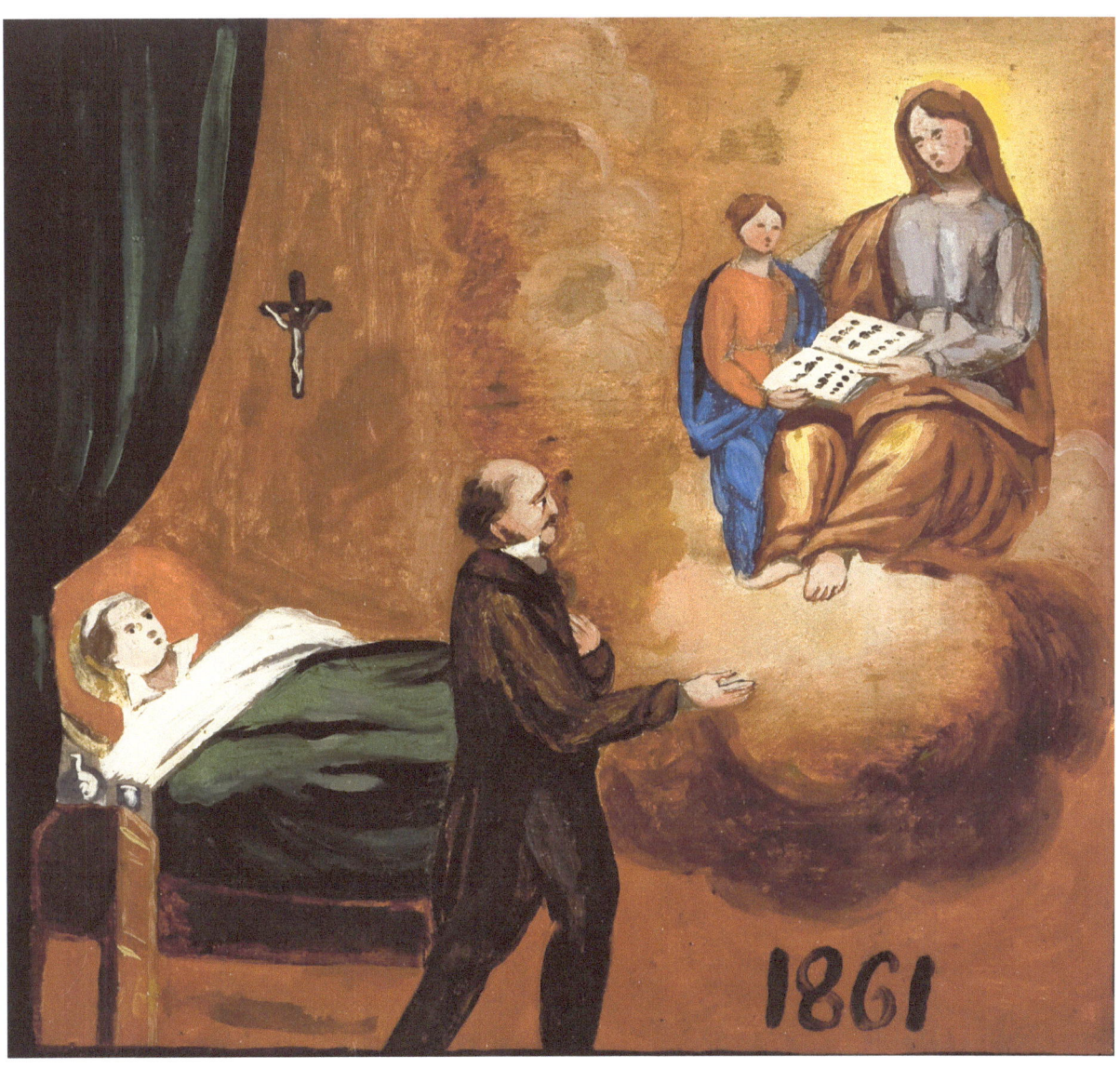

FIGURE 38

OIL ON PASTEBOARD

13¼ x 9¼ INCHES (34 x 23.5 CM)

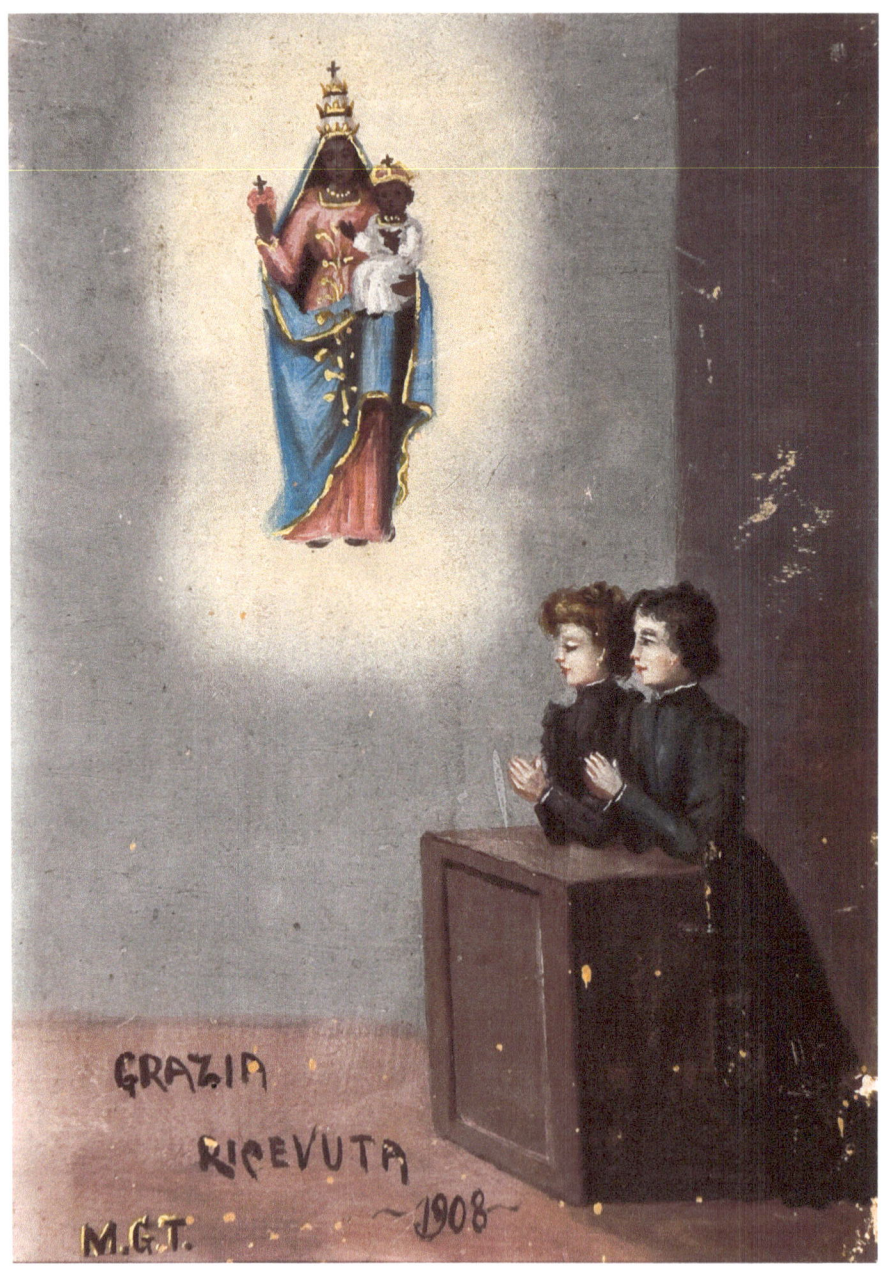

FIGURE 39

OIL ON WOOD

11 X 14½ INCHES (28 X 36.5 CM)

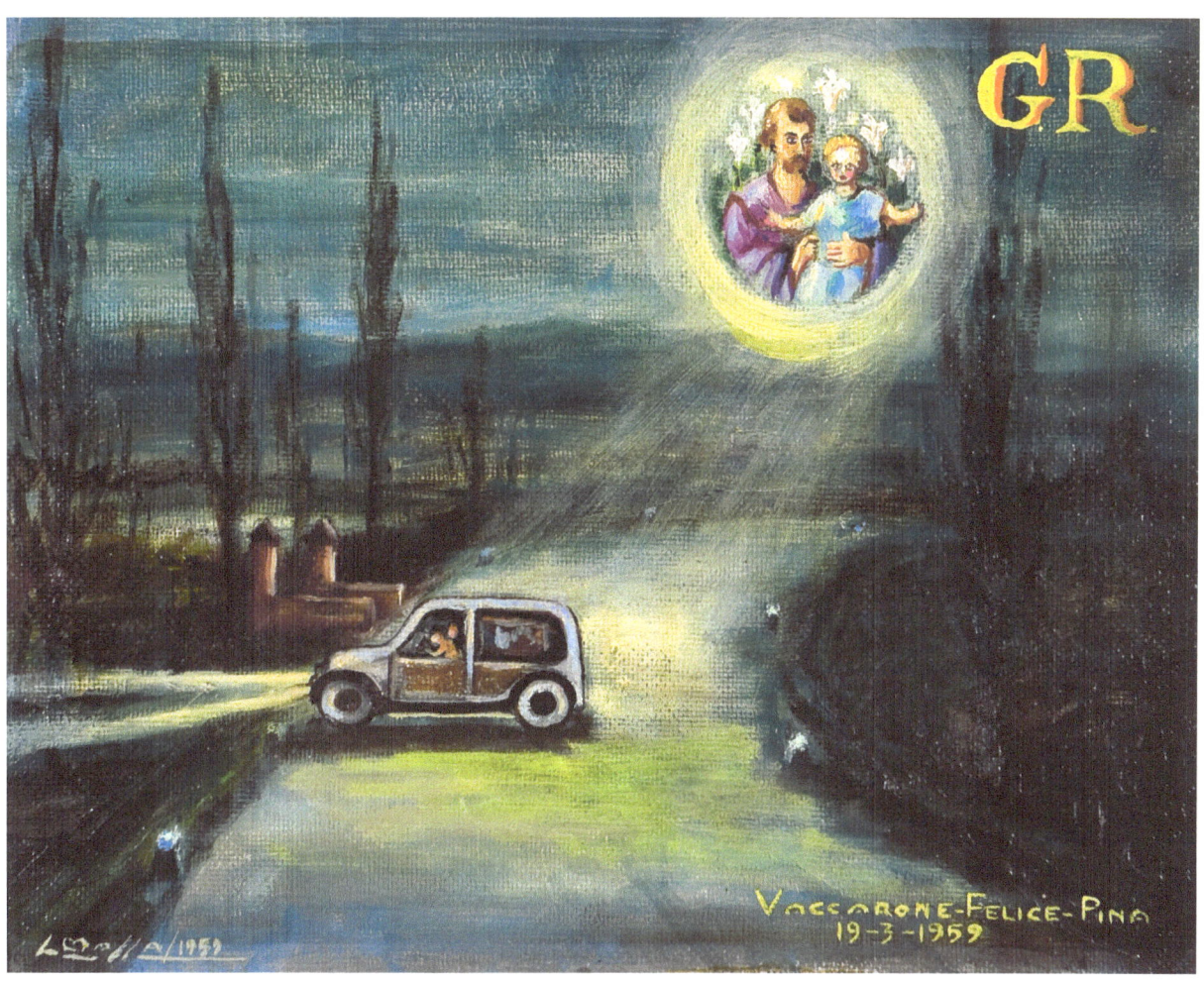

FIGURE 40

STERLING SILVER

INSCRIPTION: 15 AGOSTO 1851 / GR /

FAMIGLIA NODARI

6½ x 3¾ INCHES (16 X 9.5 CM)

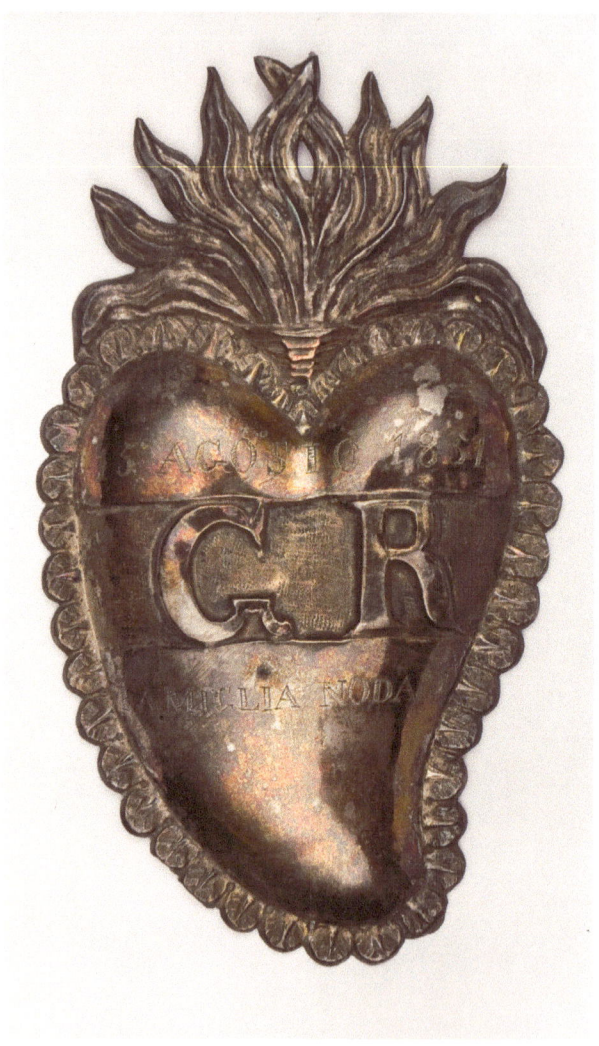

FIGURE 41

SILVERPLATE
8½ x 7 INCHES (22 x 17.5 CM)

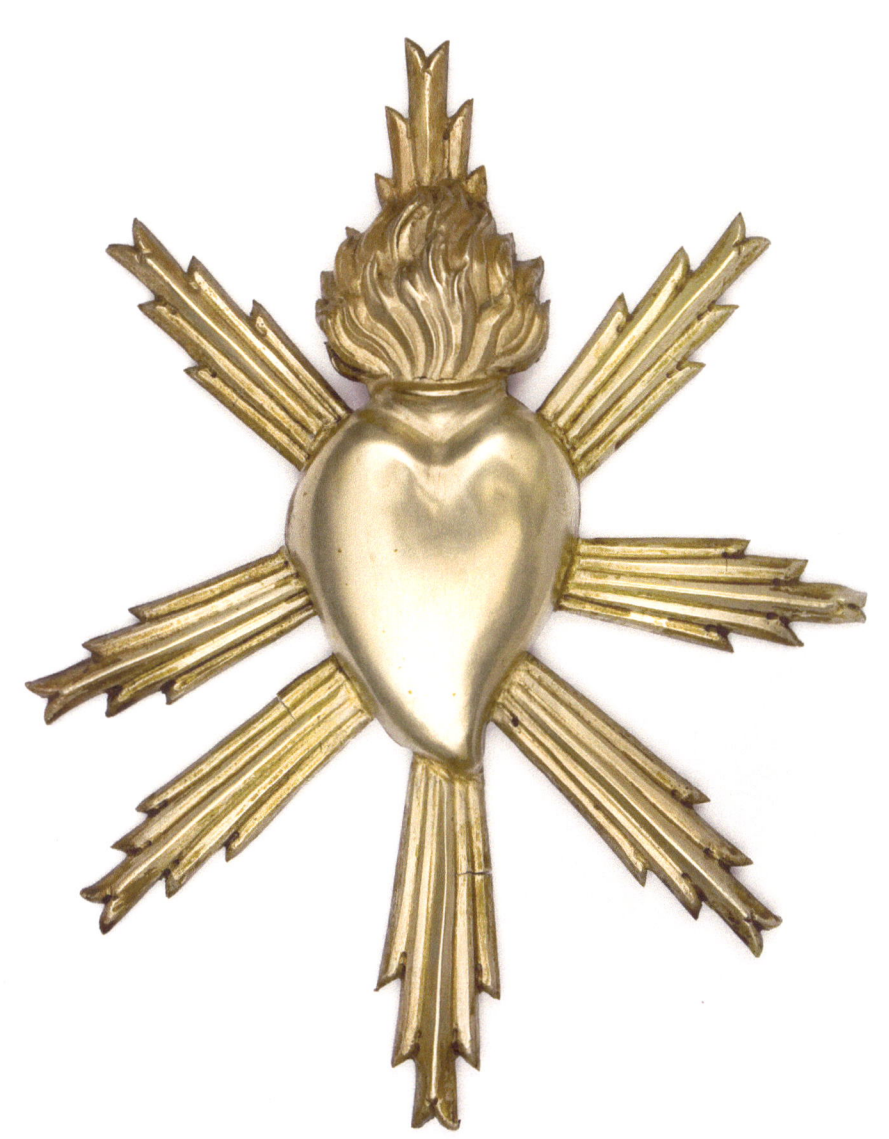

FIGURE 42

SILVERPLATE

5¼ x 1¾ INCHES (13 X 4.5 CM)

FIGURE 43

TIN, RIBBON

5 X 2 INCHES (13 X 5 CM)

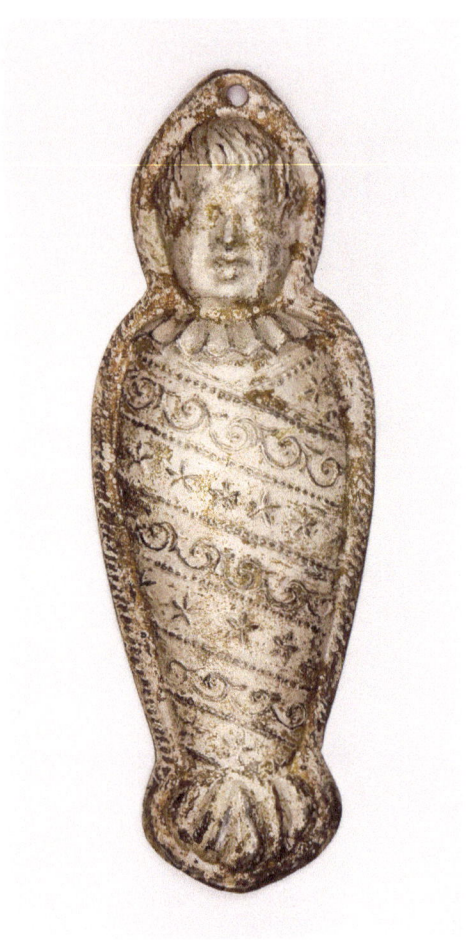

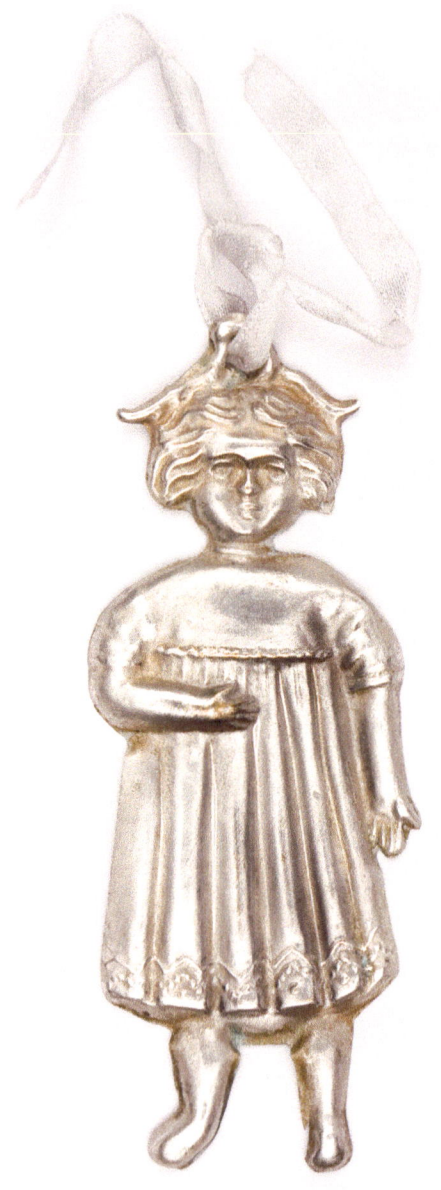

FIGURE 44

SILVERPLATE, RIBBON
5¼ X 3½ INCHES (13.5 X 9 CM)

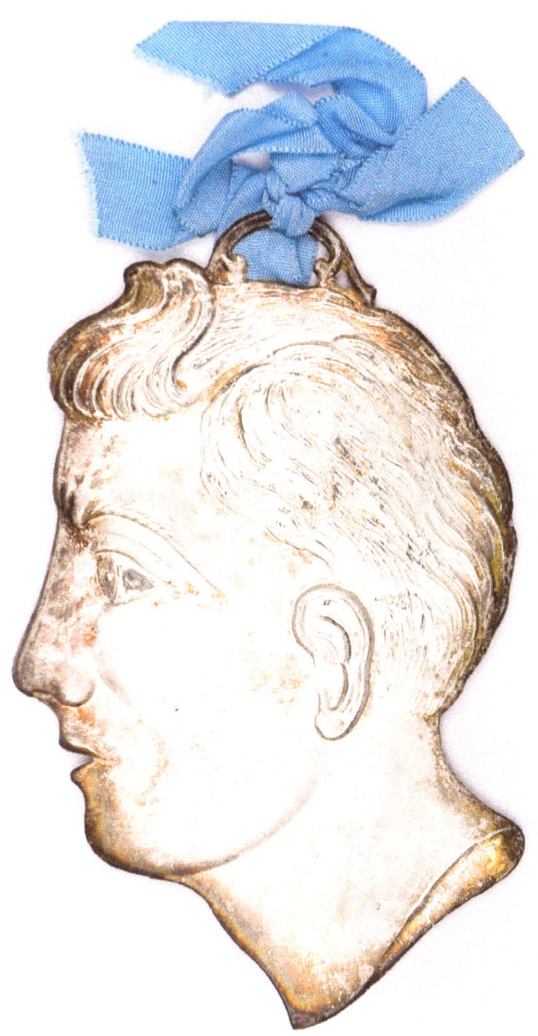

FIGURE 45

SILVERPLATE

3½ x 2¾ INCHES (9 x 7 CM)

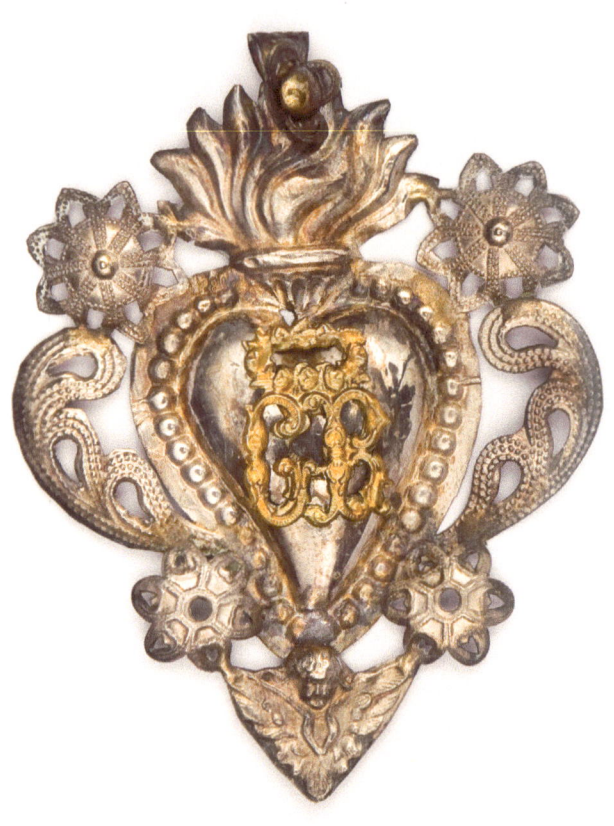

FIGURE 46

SILVERPLATE
8 x 8½ INCHES (20.5 x 22 CM)

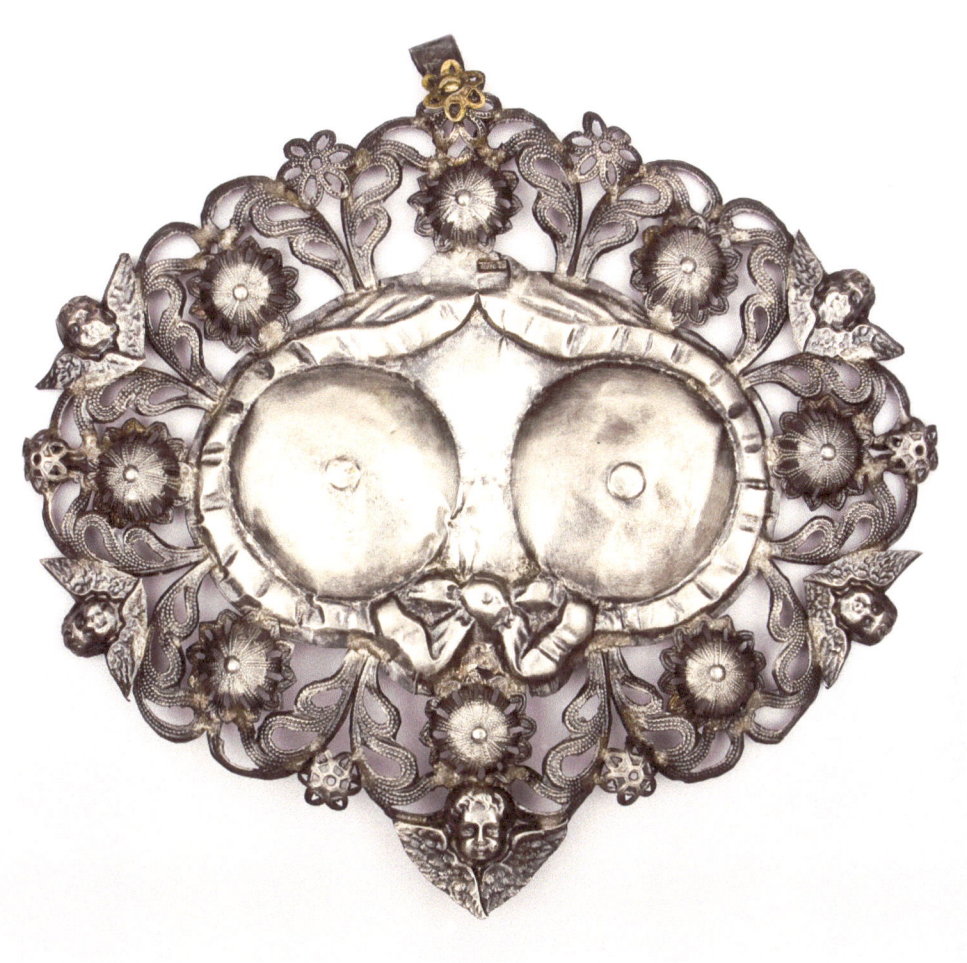

FIGURE 47

TIN

4¾ x 6¼ INCHES (12 x 16 CM)

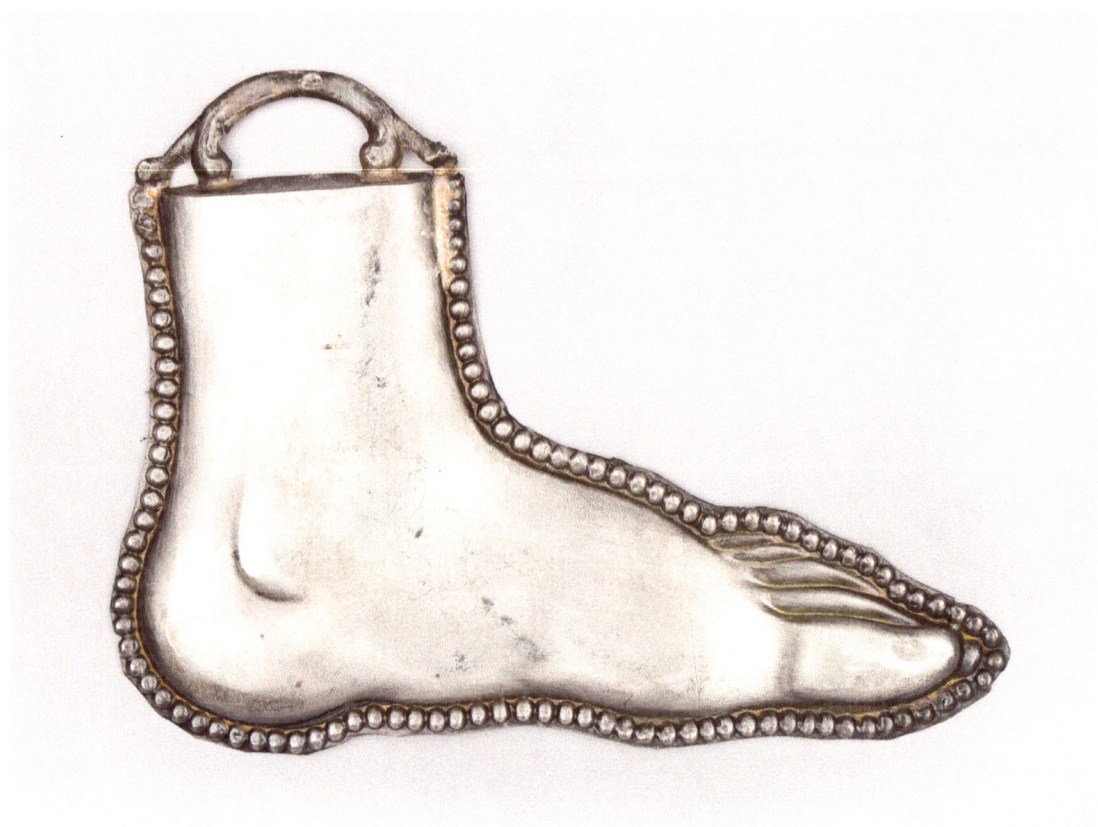

FIGURE 48

SILVERPLATE
2¾ X 4⅓ INCHES (7 X 11 CM)

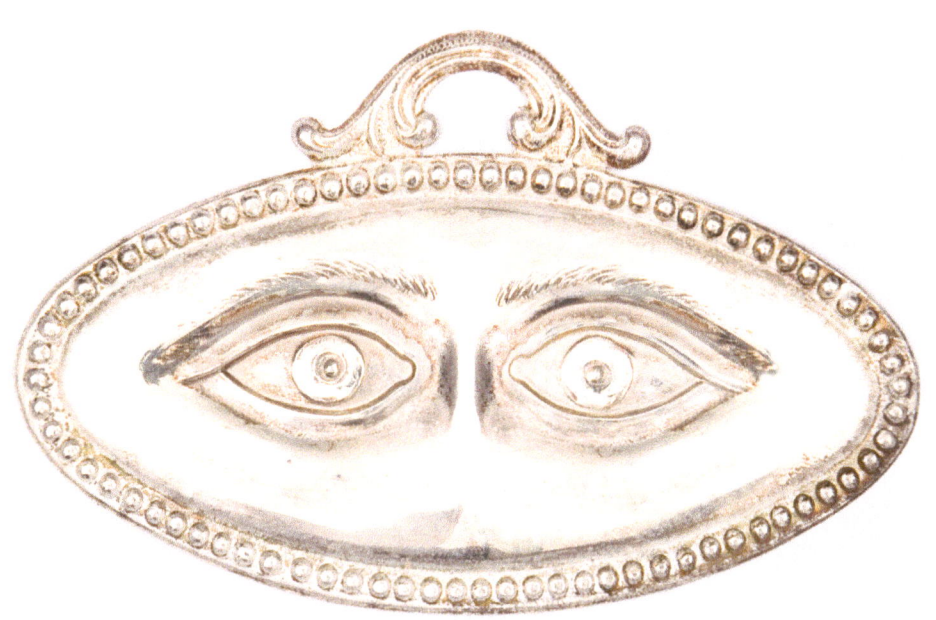

FIGURE 49

SILVERPLATE, RIBBON
4¼ x 3 INCHES (10.5 x 7.5 CM)

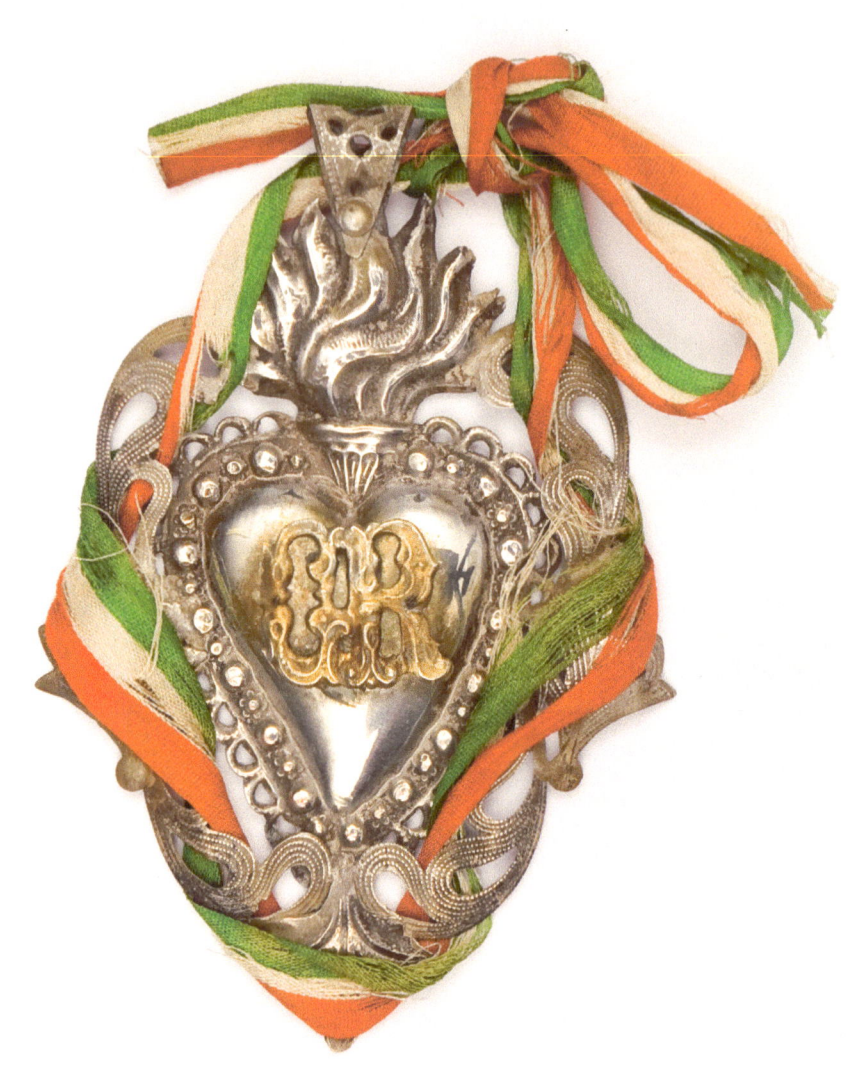

ROSANGELA BRISCESE is the coordinator for Academic and Cultural Programs at the John D. Calandra Italian American Institute, Queens College (City University of New York), where she organizes the Institute's "Philip V. Cannistraro Seminar Series in Italian American Studies," the "Writers Read" author series, the "Documented Italians" film series, exhibitions, and other special events. She is the managing editor of the Institute's journal *Italian American Review*. Briscese received her B.A. in English from Rutgers University and her graduate degree from the University of Texas at Austin's School of Information, specializing in archives and preservation. She serves on the board of trustees of the Flow Chart Foundation, which oversees poet John Ashbery's archives and collections, the board of the New Jersey Folk Festival, and the Juglaris Publication Commission.

LEONARD NORMAN PRIMIANO is professor and chair of the Department of Religious Studies at Cabrini College, and co-director of the Honors Program. He is the co-producer and co-founder of "The Father Divine Project," a multimedia documentary and video podcast about The Peace Mission Movement. Recent research and publications include an examination of the St. Joseph Day altars and the related devotional practices of Sicilian Americans in Gloucester, Massachusetts; a consideration of vernacular Catholicism in *The West Wing*; an analysis of the musical culture of Father Divine's Peace Mission Movement; a study of Roman Catholic ephemeral culture as exemplified by the holy card; and the article "'I Wanna Do Bad Things With You:' Fantasia on Themes of American Religion from the Title Sequence of HBO's *True Blood*," in the second edition of *God in the Details: American Religion in Popular Culture* (2011). Primiano currently serves on the executive board of the American Folklore Society.

JOSEPH SCIORRA is the associate director for Academic and Cultural Programs at the John D. Calandra Italian American Institute, Queens College (City University of New York). As a folklorist, he has published on religious practices, material culture, and popular music, among other topics. He is editor of the journal, *Italian American Review*, *Italian Folk: Vernacular Culture in Italian-American Lives* (2011), and *Sacred Emblems, Community Signs: Historic Flags and Religious Banners from Italian Williamsburg, Brooklyn* (2003), co-editor of poet Vincenzo Ancona's *Malidittu la lingua/Damned Language* (1990; 2010) and *Mediated Ethnicity: New Italian-American Cinema* (2010), and author of *R.I.P.: Memorial Wall Art* (1994; 2002). He has conceptualized and curated several exhibitions, including "Evviva La Madonna Nera!: Italian-American Devotion to the Black Madonna." As the avatar "Joey Skee," Sciorra is an invited blogger of "Occhio contro occhio," at www.i-italy.org.

KATE WAGLE, professor of art, is administrative director of the School of Architecture and Allied Arts at the University of Oregon in Portland. She exhibits her artwork internationally and leads workshops throughout the country and in Asia. Her work has been the subject of numerous articles and reviews, and she was awarded a regional artist fellowship from the National Endowment for the Arts. She also writes for periodicals in her field, serves on the executive committee of the National Association of Schools of Art and Design, and chaired the editorial advisory committee for *Metalsmith* magazine from 2004 to 2007. Prior to her appointment in Portland, Wagle served from 1999 to 2008 as head of the Department of Art at the University of Oregon in Eugene. She received her graduate degree in art from Arizona State University.

www.ingramcontent.com/pod-product-compliance
Lightning Source LLC
Chambersburg PA
CBHW050722180526
45159CB00003B/1106